The CALDON CANAL AND TRAMROADS

INCLUDING
THE UTTOXETER AND LEEK CANALS
AND NORTH STAFFORD RAILWAY

by

Peter Lead

THE OAKWOOD PRESS

© 1990 Oakwood Press and Peter Lead
ISBN 0 85361 404 0

First published 1979
Second enlarged edition 1990

Typeset by Gem Publishing Company, Brightwell, Wallingford, Oxfordshire.
Printed by S & S Press, Abingdon, Oxfordshire.

Dedicated to my father: Oswald John Lead, 1911–1983.

All rights reserved. No part of this book may be reproduced or transmitted in any form or by any means, electronic or mechanical, including photo-copying, recording or by any information storage and retrieval system, without permission from the Publisher in writing.

A 'bridge' of boats was constructed in 1920 when this huge boiler was delivered to the Eagle Pottery. The lad (wearing the cap) and sitting on the cabin of *Cuba* is reputed to be Stanley Matthews, later to become a legendary figure in football. The other boats in the photograph are *Westwood* and *Scotia*. *Dennis Morris*

Title page: A cast-iron milepost (near Denstone) manufactured by Rangeley and Dixon in 1820. Such mileposts replaced the earlier stone mileposts on the Caldon Canal and were the only type ever erected on the Uttoxeter Canal. *The late Peter Norton*

Published by
The OAKWOOD PRESS
P.O.Box 122, Headington, Oxford.

Contents

	Preface	3
Chapter One	**Promoting the Canal**	7
Chapter Two	**Constructing the Canal**	17
Chapter Three	**Consolidation**	21
Chapter Four	**A Period of Prosperity**	33
Chapter Five	**Decline**	37
Chapter Six	**Restoration and New Life**	41
Chapter Seven	**The Leek Canal and Rudyard Reservoir**	51
Chapter Eight	**The Uttoxeter Canal**	57
Chapter Nine	**The Caldon Low Railways**	67
Chapter Ten	**The North Stafford Railway of 1815**	85
	Bibliography	94

Abbreviations

HRL	Hanley Reference Library, Stoke-on-Trent
JHC	Journals of the House of Commons
JSIAS	Journal of the Staffordshire Industrial Archaeology Society
KEELE	University of Keele
PRO	Public Record Office
SCC	Staffordshire County Council
SRO	Staffordshire Record Office
TM	Trent and Mersey Canal
WSL	William Salt Library, Stafford

Preface to the Second Edition

The first edition of this book was published ten years ago and it represented the fruits of my research up to that time. Inevitably, new archive material has become available and this has enabled me to extend the account of the North Stafford Railway of 1815 and to correct a fundamental error concerning the dating of the last Caldon Low tramway. I have also had the opportunity to research the careers of John and Thomas Gilbert, James

Brindley and the Trent and Mersey canal system in general. Much new evidence has encouraged me to rewrite the text in its entirety, incorporating new information and reproductions of contemporary documentary sources. I am also pleased to be able to include a revised and enhanced selection of photographs, a number of which have recently come to light and are published here for the first time. As the records of the Trent and Mersey Canal Company were systematically destroyed at Stoke in the period of 1947–48, there is a striking lack of the range of records that so often survived the passing of many canal companies.

I first explored the area around Consall Forge in 1967, when the Caldon canal was just one more derelict feature amid a mysterious landscape which subtly reflected a variety of former industrial activities. From this experience grew an enduring interest in industrial archaeology which was fuelled by the late Herbert Chester. His life-long study of the Cheadle area was crowned by two important publications and without his help and guidance this book would have been much the poorer.

In common with anyone who embarks on a project of historical research, I owe a great deal to numerous librarians and archivists. I am especially grateful to the staff of the William Salt Library and the County Record Office at Stafford, particularly Dr F. Stitt (former County Archivist) and his successor Dudley Fowkes. I would also like to acknowledge my gratitude to the following who have helped in a variety of ways: Anne Bayliss; C.M. Beardmore; the late Professor S.H. Beaver; Tom Billings; Will Billings; Grahame Boyes; John Challinor; the late Norman A. Cope; Robert Copeland; the late Olive A. Dale; Dr A.E. and Mrs E.M. Dodd; N. Emery, Honorary Librarian, North Staffordshire Field Club; the Editor, *Evening Sentinel*; M.H. Finch, British Waterways Board; R. Fletcher; Ben Fradley; Charles Hadfield; Dr J.R. Hollick; Alan Jeffery; Robert Milner; Dennis B. Morris; W.G. Myatt; the late Peter Norton; the late Hugh Oliver; H.L. Podmore; Lindsey Porter; Francis Pratt, British Waterways Board; Gordon Rattenbury; Philip Riden; Dr John Robey; Tim Sidway, British Waterways Board; B.H. Snow; Dr Hugh Torrens; Frank Underwood; E.J.D. Warrilow and Derek Wheelhouse.

A lot of confusion exists about whether it should be 'Caldon Low' or 'Cauldon Lowe'. The most recent Ordnance Survey 1:50,000 map (sheet 119) gives: 'Cauldon' for the village; 'Caldon Low' for the quarries and 'Cauldon Lowe' for the hill south of the A52. For the sake of clarity, I have standardised my spelling on the first edition of the one-inch Ordnance Survey of England and Wales (1836), which uses 'Caldon' throughout.

January 1990

Peter Lead
Stone, Staffordshire

The entrance to the Bedford Street Locks, Etruria seen here in 1940. The bridge was in the process of being demolished after being hit by a bomb, intended for the nearby Shelton steelworks. *Frank Underwood*

The Etruria Lock and Check Office, 1892. This carefully posed group of canal officials were (*left to right*): Mr Corbishley, the canal engineer; Richard Leese, canal agent at Etruria; and H.C. James who worked in the check office. *Frank Underwood*

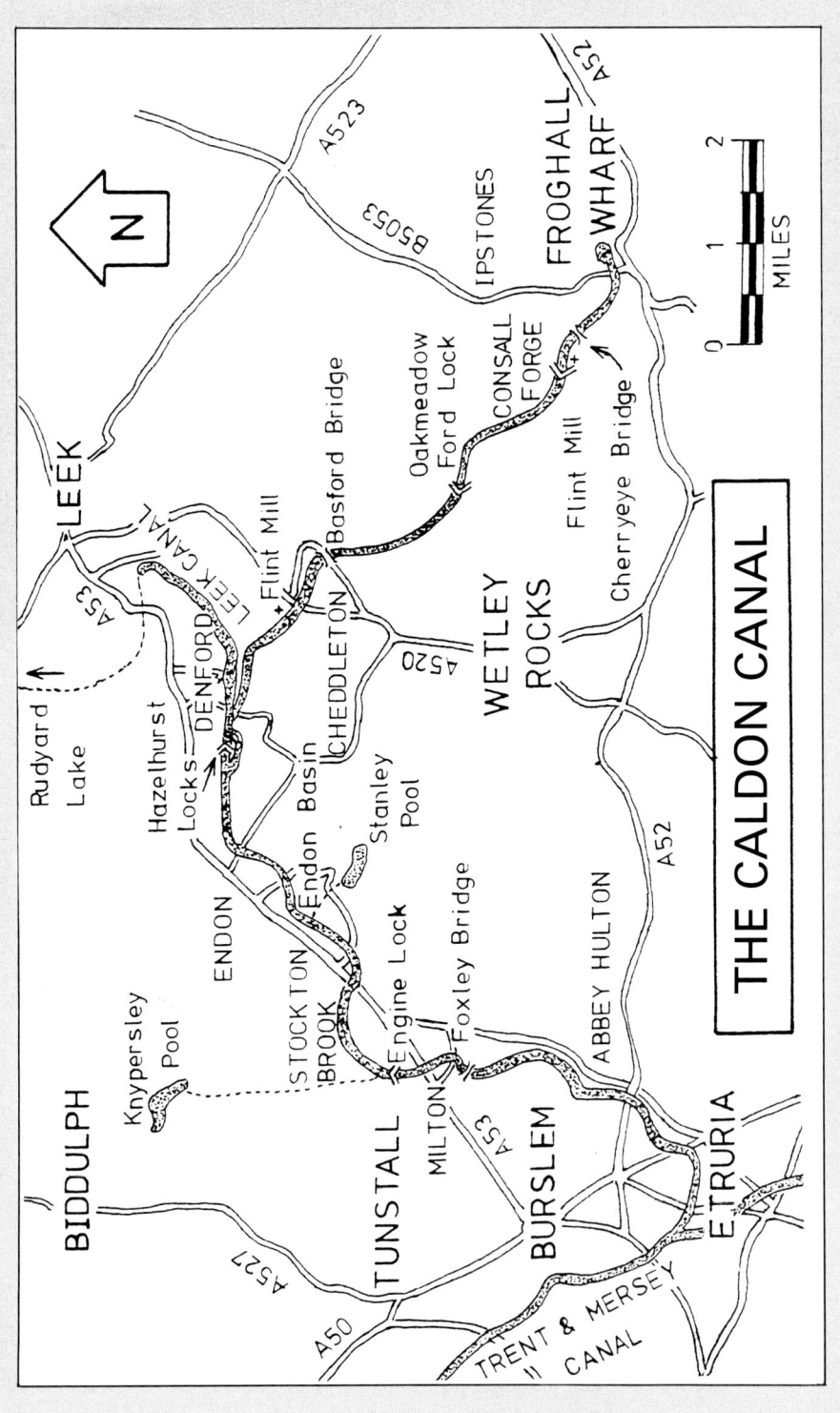

Chapter One
Promoting the Canal

As the minute books of the Trent and Mersey Canal Company were destroyed it has proved difficult to identify the prime reason for the promotion of the Caldon Canal. The explanation usually given is that the canal company wished to enjoy the additional revenue to be derived from the tolls on the traffic that would emanate from the Caldon Low limestone quarries. Obviously, John and Thomas Gilbert, in company with their fellow quarry operators, were keen to expand production at Caldon Low which at the time only served a limited local market.

John and Thomas Gilbert had long been associated with James Brindley on a number of levels. They had employed him in their own right as coal-masters and mining entrepreneurs; they were his immediate superiors in his employment with the Duke of Bridgewater; and they were his business partners in at least one mining venture. Therefore, it is not surprising that they enlisted his help in the promotion of a branch canal to serve the Caldon Low quarries. Brindley was surveyor-general to the Trent and Mersey Canal Company and during the late summer of 1772 he made one of his 'ochilor surveys' towards Caldon Low. Such surveys involved him in riding along likely routes before making a set of recommendations to the canal company, who would then commission a more detailed survey. Samuel Smiles relates a local tradition that asserts that during this particular surveying trip Brindley got a soaking in a sudden storm, caught a chill and having reached the village of Ipstones was put into a damp bed.[1]

These exertions coupled with years of overwork and untreated diabetes brought on his final illness. The progressive Dr Erasmus Darwin was brought to attend him, but it was too late. Josiah Wedgwood's letters chronicle a steady decline which culminated in his death on 27th September, 1772.[2] Considering the sudden and incapacitating nature of his final illness it is highly unlikely that he was able to make even the most rudimentary report; but within four months of his passing Josiah Wedgwood was able to describe an amended plan behind which can be seen the influence of John Gilbert. This plan involved building a branch from Etruria, through Leek to Caldon Low. Inclined planes were to be used in place of locks; the canal was to be a mere 12 ft wide; and tub boats capable of carrying only 5 tons were to be used instead of the then already standardised narrow-boats.[3]

More precise technical details were given by John Sneyd of Belmont Hall, in a letter he wrote to Sir Joseph Banks, who had an estate nearby at Kingsley. Written early in January 1773 it informs Banks that:

> We are going to petition Parliament for a navigable Canal from ye Potteries beyond Leek principally for Coal and Lime carriage wch. be executed at a very moderate Expence by means of an Invention one of our Moorlanders has hit off for drawing loaded Barges of 7 or 8 Ton up an inclined plane wch rises 13 inches in ye yard instead of Locks. This has been tryed at large and a Boy of 12 years old draws them up with ye greatest ease by a common capstan. The boat swims over a 4 wheeled carriage wch sinks to ye bottom of ye canal it is then fastened upon it and so drawn over.[4]

A potters' millers at Etruria Vale in 1948. The narrow boat is *Durban* which belonged to George Mellor and Company, owners of the mill. *The late Stanley Beaver*

Ware being loaded aboard the *Milton Queen* at Eastwood, Hanley in 1974. This boat belongs to Johnson Brothers, part of the earthenware division of the Wedgwood Group. *Josiah Wedgwood and Sons Ltd.*

The *Milton Queen* heading for Milton with a load of earthenware. This journey takes about one hour and maintains the traditional link between the Wedgwood group and the local canal system. *Josiah Wedgwood and Sons Ltd*

The pioneer boat built by Johnson Brothers, the *Milton Maid* has turned turtle on a number of occasions. This picture taken in 1975 near Birches Head Road, shows workmen recovering earthenware from the canal. *Evening Sentinel*

It would be most satisfying to know who the 'Moorlander' was and the obvious candidate is John Gilbert, who had been born and brought up at Cotton Hall, four miles away from Sneyd's home. Despite Sneyd's assertion that this was the 'invention' of a local man, it is known for certain that it was nothing of the kind. W.A. McCutcheon in *The Canals of the North of Ireland* has shown that Davies Dukart proposed to build a canal on very similar lines from the Tyronne Navigation to a nearby colliery. William Chapman described how Dukart had

> . . . a cradle or frame with four wheels, brought under his boats; upon which, over a double railway, they alternatively ascended and descended. . . . (H)e made use of a horse-gin to draw his boats upon the ridge terminating the upper level.[5]

Clearly the two descriptions have much in common, although the use of a 'capstan' is reminiscent of the 'windlass' system used in the Netherlands at this time. Perhaps Sneyd's letter is a description of a hybrid system, based on Dukart's work. It is known that Dukart visited the Duke of Bridgewater's estate at Worsley in August 1768; and that he shortly afterwards inspected the construction work on the Trent and Mersey Canal including the Harecastle Tunnel.[6] John Gilbert was steward (or estate agent) to the Duke of Bridgewater at Worsley and he may well have had discussions with Dukart during his visit. The reference by Josiah Wedgwood to tub boats capable of carrying 5 tons is also of great significance. For on the Donnington Wood Canal (engineered by John Gilbert between 1765 and 1768) the tub boats were capable of carrying exactly the same tonnage, although the system of transfer between levels involved an early version of containerisation.[7]

All that has been said so far tends to emphasise the interests of the quarry owners and their desire to gain a direct link with the growing national canal network. Yet it is almost certain that the canal company were eventually persuaded to undertake the construction of the Caldon Canal due to the almost insatiable need for more water on the summit level at Etruria. A management committee memorandum (dated 8th November, 1774) recognised the urgent need to obtain more water before the main line was opened throughout to traffic. They ordered that: 'Foxley Brook water be brought by canal or a trench into our canal to increase our water and that Mr Henshaw (Hugh Henshall) take a survey of the premises and ye expences attending ye same'.[8] The urgency of this matter was stressed a year later, when John Sparrow (clerk to the canal company) wrote of the need for 'a plentiful supply of water' to 'the numerous locks on the summit level'.[9] As will be seen later, the Caldon Canal and the various reservoirs built adjacent to its circuitous route largely met this need and prompted one writer to describe the 'aqueous supplies drawn from the neighbouring Moor-lands, descending into the AORTA of inland commerce'.[10]

Josiah Wedgwood viewed a proposed route for the canal in October 1775, one month after announcing that 'we (the canal company) are begun upon it in earnest'. In a letter to his nine year old son, he describes how the course of the canal was to run 'parallel with the road from Leek to Ashbourne for some miles' until it reached the western edge of Caldon Low.[11] By November of the same year this plan had been finally approved and an estimate prepared.

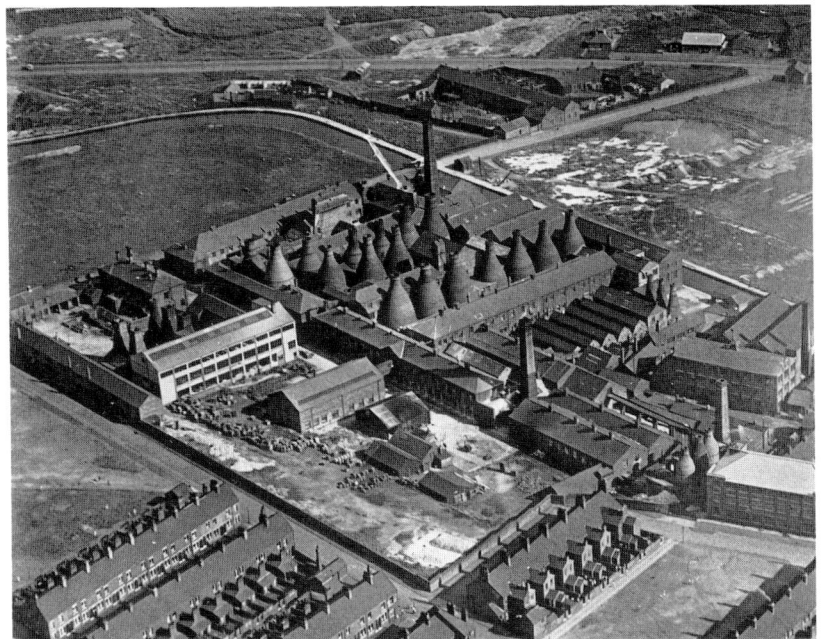

A fine aerial view of the Eagle Pottery, Hanley taken during the late 1920s. These works represent a classic example of canalside location with the disturbed ground on the other side of the canal marking the site of a former colliery.   *J. & G. Meakin Ltd*

The Caldon Canal at Birches Head about 1905. The maintenance boat is of great interest as it is built along the same lines as the Worsley mine boats and may have been used previously in the side-tunnels, inside Harecastle Hill.   *Dennis Morris*

More precise details of this route emerge from a petition presented to Parliament on 12th February, 1776. This petition describes a branch canal from the main canal near Hanley, via Norton to Cheddleton. From this point a 'railed way' was to run to Sharpcliff (above the Combes Valley) and from there another stretch of canal would complete the route to the western side of the Caldon Low quarries. This would have run 'parallel with the road from Leek to Ashbourne' as Josiah Wedgwood noted, but a mile and a half to the south-west of this turnpike road.

This same petition also mentions 'proper surveys lately taken' which suggests that other routes had been considered by the canal company; but it was clear that Leek was to be bypassed.[12] This prompted real and lasting anger in many of the townsfolk of that town; one of whom lamented nearly 20 years later that the 'Froghall Canal had prevented the building of a canal to Leek'.[13] Further discontent was expressed in a petition presented against the company's proposals by John Bagnall, Benjamin Yardley and William Adams, owners of mills at Bucknall, Milton and Cheddleton. They all feared that the canal would rob them of their water supply and argued that this would cause local people to have to carry their corn further afield for milling.[14]

Their opposition appears to have been simply brushed aside for the next set of proposals retained the elements that would have affected mill-owners, but made a very radical change with regard to the final section between Cheddleton and Caldon Low. It was proposed that the canal would proceed through Consall Forge to Froghall; and a 'Rail-way' be built from there to the Caldon Low quarries. These proposals were put before Parliament in another petition, dated 18th April, 1776; and they were to represent the plan that was to be finally approved.[15] At the committee stage, Hugh Henshall (who had succeeded his brother-in-law James Brindley as surveyor-general to the company) gave evidence that most of the landowners were in agreement with this latest plan. Parliament gave its approval to the new route on 24th April, 1776 and the Act received the Royal Assent on 13th May of the same year.[16]

The decision to take the canal through the gorge near Consall Forge cannot be explained in terms of comparative landowner resistance, or engineering considerations. The company had ignored or overcome the relatively weak opposition from local landowners and the owners of the named mills; whilst major engineering problems awaited them between Consall Wood and the wharf site near Froghall. The company's financial problems were to prove crucial in making this decision, especially since the main line of the canal was still not complete. The Act itself provides the real reason for the final change as it relates how a group of colliery owners had agreed to advance the sum of £5,000 towards the cost of building the canal. These men were developing collieries in Kingsley, Cheadle and Froghall; so it was clearly in their best interest to have the canal follow the route that it did. Edward Leigh (a sub-tenant of the Gilbert brothers in the Woodhead Colliery), Thomas Mytton and John Beech were the individual coalmasters who offered the loan to the canal company. They were each to receive interest at 4½ per cent and half the tolls from coal produced south of River Churnet during the period of the loan. The mines north of the Churnet in Farley and Cotton had been leased by John Gilbert in 1767 and he used them to supply the limekilns at Caldon Low.[17] The Bill family of Farley Hall (related to the Gilberts by marriage) also favoured the Cheddleton to Froghall route as they intended to convert the old ironworks at Consall Forge into a flint mill.[18]

The canal company made agreements with the owners and tenants of the various limestone quarries around Caldon Low. This group consisted of: Thomas Gilbert, John Gilbert, Richard Hill, George Smith, Sampson Whieldon, Henry Copestake, Robert Bill and Henry Wooliscroft; a few of these men also held shares in the canal company. The company agreed to pay 7d. per ton for broken limestone, but reserved the right to work the quarries themselves if the supply failed to keep pace with their requirements. The company was to build the main railway between Froghall and Caldon Low, the branch lines into the quarries being the sole concern of the owners and tenants.[19]

References

1 Samuel Smiles, *Lives of the Engineers*, Vol. I, p. 470.
2 K.E. Farrer, *Correspondence of Josiah Wedgwood*, Vol. II, pp. 97–103.
3 Wedgwood Papers, Keele: J. Wedgwood to T. Bentley, 23rd January, 1773.
4 PRO: Banks' Letters — BC1–30.
5 William Chapman, *Observations on the various systems of Canal Navigation*, p. 6.
6 W.H. Chaloner, 'James Brindley and his remuneration as a Canal Engineer', *Trans of the Lancashire and Cheshire Antiquarian Society*, Vols 75 & 76 (1965–1966), pp. 226–228.
7 *Abraham Rees's Manufacturing Industry (1819–20)*; edited by N. Cossons (1972), Vol. I, p. 392.
8 WSL: HM 37/19.
9 SRO: D554/162.
10 John Ward, *History of the Borough of Stoke-upon-Trent*, (1843), p. 388.
11 Wedgwood Papers, Keele: J. Wedgwood to his son John, 5th October, 1775.
12 JHC, XXXV, p. 548.
13 *Derby Mercury*, (Derby Reference Library), 14th November, 1793.
14 JHC, XXXV, pp. 663–4.
15 Ibid., p. 706.
16 WSL: HM 37/19.
17 SRO: D240/K/D.
18 SRO: D239/M/1212 and 1217.
19 SRO: D239/M/2138 and 2139.

AN ABSTRACT *of the Act of* 16th. GEO, III. *for enabling the* COMPANY *of* PROPRIETORS *of the* NAVIGATION *from the* TRENT *to the* MERSEY, *to make a navigable Canal, from the said* NAVIGATION, *on the South side of* HARECASTLE, *in the County of* STAFFORD, *to* FROGHALL, *and a* RAILWAY *from thence to or near* CALDON, *in the said County, and to make other* RAILWAYS.

THE Act recites the Act of the 6th. Geo. III. for making a navigable Canal, from the *Trent* to the *Merley,* and that in pursuance of the said Act, and of two others, of the 10th. and 15th. Geo. III. the *Company* have proceeded to make the said Canal &c. and have nearly completed the same. That by a Survey lately made, it appears that a branch may be made, from the said Canal on the South side of *Harecastle,* by *Hanley, Norton,* and *Chedleton,* to *Froghall,* from whence a *Railway* may be made, to or near several Lime-works, and Lime-stone Quarries, at or near *Caldon,* &c. and that the *Company* are willing to undertake the same.——IT IT THEREFORE ENACTS, That the *Company* shall and may, and they are thereby authorized and empowered, to make the said Canal and Railway, and also other Railways, from the proposed Canal and Railway, to the several Coalmines, and Limestone Quarries, lying near the Course of the said Canal and Railway, making satisfaction &c. in manner therein mentioned.

THE said Canal and Railway are directed to be made pursuant to a Plan and Book of reference, certified by the Speaker of the House of Commons &c.

THE Commissioners appointed by the 6th. Geo. III. and several other Persons named in this Act, are appointed Commissioners, for adjusting all differences, between the *Company,* and the Owners of Lands &c.

IN Consideration of the expences attending the execution of the Works hereby authorized, the *Company,* are empowered to take, and receive to their own use, the following Rates or Duties, *(viz.)* 1d. ¾. per Mile, for every Ton of Coal, Stone, Timber, and other Goods, which shall be navigated, carried, or conveyed, upon the said Canal, Railways, or passages, and so in proportion for any quantity, more or less, than a Ton, and for any distance, more or less than one Mile, and also the further Sum of one halfpenny *per* Mile, for every Ton of Coals, Cannel, and Slack, brought from any of the Coalmines, within the Parishes of *Kingsley,* and *Cheadle,* lying on the South side of the River *Churnett,* which shall be navigated, carried, or conveyed, upon any part of the said Canal and Railway, between the Turnpike Road in *Chedleton,* and the termination of the said Railway, near *Caldon* aforesaid, and so in proportion &c.

THE *Company* are authorized to borrow at legal or less Interest, on the Credit of the Undertaking, and the Tolls, and Duties, granted by the Act, any Sum, or Sums of Money, not exceeding 25,000*l.* and to assign over the same, or any part thereof, as a Security for the Money so to be borrowed, by the form of an Assignment prescribed in the Act. And all Persons to whom such Assignments shall be made, shall be equally intitled to their proportion of the said Tolls, Rates, and Duties, according to the respective Sums by them advanced, without any preference by reason of priority of Assignment, which Securities may be transferred, from time to time, in like manner as the Securities made under the former Acts, and the Interest of the Money borrowed is to be paid half yearly in preference to any dividends to be made to the *Proprietors.*

THE Act recites, that the said proposed Canal, and Railway, will be of great advantage to the several Proprietors of Coalmines, in the Parishes of *Kingsley,* and *Cheadle,* on the South side of the *Churnett near Froghall;* and in Consideration thereof, and as an inducement to the *Company* to make the Canal by *Froghall,* several Proprietors of Coalmines, therein named, had agreed to advance to the *Company,* on or before the 25th *December* next, the Sum of 5000*l.* to be laid out in the Works on the Security after mentioned. It therefore Enacts, That one half of the Tolls arising from Coals, Cannel, and Slack, produced in the said Parishes, South of the *Churnett,* which should be carried on the Canal, and Railway, between the Turnpike Road in *Chedleton,* and the Termination of the Railway, near *Caldon,* shall be vested in the said Coal Proprietors, (redeemable by the *Company* as after mentioned) and shall be paid by the *Company,* to the said Coal Proprietors by four equal quarterly payments, until the said Sum of 5000*l.* together with Interest at 4*l.* 10*s.* per Cent, per Annum, shall be paid; and that the *Company* shall out of the Money to arise under this Act pay to the said Coal Proprietors Interest for the said 5000*l.* from the time of advancing the same, 'till the said Canal and Railway, between *Chedleton,* and *Caldon,* shall be completed, after the rate of 4*l.* 10*s. per Cent, per Annum,* in case the same shall not be completed, in two Years from the passing the Act : The *Company* are empowered to redeem the said Tolls last mentioned, at any time upon payment of the said 5000*l.* and Interest, or so much as shall remain due on balance.

Recites also, that there are great quantities of excellent Lime stone, in the Parishes of *Caldon* and *Alveton,* lying near the termination of the said intended Railway, which may be conveyed by means of the said intended Canal, and Railway, and of the *Navigation* from the *Trent* to the *Mersey,* to a great extent, and the price of Lime will thereby be much reduced, which will greatly contribute to the improvement of Land, and be highly beneficial to the Public.—That the *Company* in order to ascertain the price of Lime-stone, and make those advantages, general and permanent, had made a

contract

Reproduced by courtesy of the Staffordshire Record Office

contract in writing, with *Thomas Gilbert, John Gilbert, Richard Hill, George Smith, Sampson Whieldon, Henry Copestake, Robert Bill,* and *William Woolscroft*, being Proprietors of different Quarries of Lime-stone, by which they had agreed, yearly and every Year, for ever hereafter, to deliver to the *Company*, or to such Person or Persons, and at such time and times, as the *Company* or their Clerk should nominate, and appoint, such quantities of good and merchantable Lime-stone, ready got and broke, in the Pits where got (as near as conveniently may be to the Railway intended to be carried to the said Quarries) as the said *Company*, or their Clerk shoulddirect, at the rate of 7*d. per* Ton, each Ton to consist of 21*C* at 120*lb.* to the Hundred; (of which Quantity, Notice is to be given before the last day of *October* in the preceding Year) and if the said Lime-stone Proprietors should neglect or refuse to deliver such quantities, it should be lawful for the *Company*, and such Persons as they should appoint, to enter into the Quarries and get such quantities of Lime-stone, as they should think proper, paying after the rate of 2*d.* a Ton for the same, and the *Company* agreed, as soon as might be, to make proper Railways to the Face of each Lime-stone Pit.

AND RECITING, that said *John Gilbert, Richard Hill, George Smith,* and *Sampson Whieldon,* are only Lessees under the Earl of *Shrewsbury*, who was seized of the Freehold, and had agreed that the said Contract should remain binding upon him, and his Heirs, and that the *Company* had made such Contract, with intent to serve the Public with Lime-stone, on the most reasonable Terms.

THE said Agreement is by the Act confirmed, and it is by the Act directed, that the said Lime shall be got and provided, by the Proprietors thereof, at the rate aforesaid, in such Proportions as shall be agreed upon amongst them, and approved of by the *Company*, before the last day of *September* for the Year then next ensuing, and in default thereof, in the Proportions following, (*viz.*) two 5*th* parts thereof by the Earl of *Shrewsbury* or his Lessees out of the Quarry lying in the Parish of *Alveton* ; one 5*th* part thereof out of the Lands of the said *Thomas Gilbert*, called the *Low-pieces*, one other 5*th* part thereof, out of the Lands of the said *Henry Copestake*, called *Hemings-Low*, or *Caldon-Low* ; and the remaining 5*th* part thereof out of the Lands of the said *Robert Bill, Sampson Whieldon,* and *William Woolscroft*, called the *Quarter piece*, all lying in the Parish of *Caldon* : AND to the intent the Public may be supplied with Punctuality, the *Company* are required, to direct one of their Clerks, to provide a Book and make entries, of the quantities of Lime-stone, which any Person shall order (which order shall be given on or before the last day of *September*) for Stone to be delivered in the then succeeding Year, and the *Company* are to notify such orders to the Lime-stone Proprietors, on or before the 27*th. October* then next following.

order to be given for less than 100 Tons, and a deposite made of 2*d.* a Ton. The said Stone to be delivered in manner following, (*viz.*) Any quantity between 100 and 300 Tons, within any time to be named in the order not sooner than two Months ; between 300 and 600 Tons, within any time not sooner than three Months ; between 600 and 1000 Tons, within any time not sooner than five Months ; and any quantity exceeding 1000 in manner following, (*viz*) one 4*th* part before 1*st. January,* one other 4*th* part before 1*st. April,* one other 4*th* part before 1*st. July,* and the remaining 4*th* part before 1*st. October*. Persons may order any quantity of Stone, at any other times, making a deposite of 3*d.* a Ton, Deposites are to be returned if Stone is not delivered pursuant to order, together with a Sum equal to the deposite as a forfeiture, and in case the Person ordering the Stone, shall not carry it away according to the direction of the Act, he forfeits his deposite. And in case of neglect or default in the Proprietors of Lime-stone, ordered before the last day of *September*, the *Company* or Persons to whom such Stone was to be delivered, may enter the Quarries and get the quantity required paying 2*d.* a Ton only.

THERE are Clauses, to prevent water being wasted on the *Navigation* from the *Trent* to the *Mersey*, by Vessels loaden with Lime-stone. To regulate the manner of drawing the water at *Cunsal Forge*. For preserving the Water of the River *Churnett*, and for extending the Powers of the former Acts (except such as are hereby altered) to the Works to be executed by this Act.

N. B. By means of the proposed *Navigation* Lime will be sold and delivered as follows, (*viz.*)

		per Ton.	per Ton.		per Ton.
		l. s. d.	*l. s. d.*		*l. s. d.*
At *Shelton,*	Where it	1 : 0 : 0	0 : 10 : 0		0 : 10 : 0
At *Trentham,*	is now	1 : 0 : 0	It will 0 : 10 : 10		0 : 9 : 2
At *Stone,*	sold at	1 : 0 : 0	be sold 0 : 11 : 8	Saving	0 : 8 : 4
At *Sandon,*		1 : 0 : 0	at 0 : 12 : 6		0 : 7 : 6
At *Haywood,*		1 : 0 : 0	0 : 13 : 4		0 : 6 : 8

And at several other Places in Proportion.

1771.

☞ THE order which was made at the *General Assembly* the 26*th.* March last, concerning the payment of Interest, having been misunderstood, this opportunity is taken of informing the *Proprietors* that the half Years Interest which became due the 18*th. September* last, will be forthwith paid to such *Proprietors* as have not already received it, either at Mr. *Stevenson's*, in *Queen-Street, Cheapside*, LONDON, or at Mr. *Stevenson's*, in *STAFFORD*.

The narrow boat *Havelock* in one of the Stockton Brook locks in 1939. At this time the boat was owned by Thomas Bolton and Sons and was used to bring coal slack to their Froghall Works.
E.J.D. Warrillow

The so called 'Endon Tip' designed by J.H. Coleman and seen here under construction in the workshops of the North Staffordshire Railway Company at Stoke.
J.R. Hollick/Manifold Collection

Chapter Two
Constructing the Canal

Exactly one month after the Act received the Royal Assent, the canal company's management committee met at Stone on 13th June, 1776. Thomas Gilbert M.P. was in the chair and the committee examined and agreed the estimated cost of £23,000 for the canal and railway, including the £5,000 promised by the colliery owners. The money was to be raised in the form of a subscription and those taking up shares were to receive interest at 4½ per cent.[1]

A start on the work of construction was made shortly after this meeting. Doubtless the desperate need for more water on the summit level at Etruria became increasingly more urgent as the main line neared completion. It is now clear that it took a little over two years to build the Caldon Canal, which corresponds with the estimate written into the Act.[2] Nevertheless a great deal of confusion has arisen over the actual date of the opening as no official ceremony was performed, or at least no record of one has survived. Opinion has been divided amongst modern writers. Some have taken John Farey's date of 1777 and others have accepted Charles Hadfield's educated guess of 1779.[3] John Farey states positively that: 'the whole line (the Trent and Mersey Canal), and the branch to Caldon Low was completed and opened in May 1777'. This statement can be verified with regard to the Trent and Mersey Canal itself, for William Bill (a committee member) wrote on 5th May, 1777 that: 'the canal will be completed in 3 weeks to 1 month's time'.[4] However, in the case of the Caldon Canal, Farey was quite clearly wrong. The Sneyd Papers clearly show that no tolls were collected on the Caldon Canal during 1777, although they were being paid by boatmen on the Trent and Mersey Canal itself.[5] Farey's dating of other engineering works was not always so positive, for when he wrote about the first Caldon Low Railway elsewhere he offers a date for the opening in '1777 or 1778'.[6]

If the evidence for completion in 1777 is unacceptable, then the evidence for the 1779 dating is equally so. Charles Hadfield explains how he arrived at his date:

> A letter of 9th January, 1780 from Edward Bill to Edward Sneyd says that tonnage on the branch from the opening to 18th December, 1779 was £896. Given that the quarterly tolls in 1783 were some £500, but on the other hand that the tramroad had to be repaired we can guess a date early in 1779.

Charles Hadfield's statement only hints at his method of estimation but it has been accepted by many writers without question. The quoted figure for 1783 is very misleading, as is shown by the following figures from the same documentary source which gives the total tolls collected on the Caldon Canal for the two years before 1783:

From Midsummer 1780 to Midsummer 1781 £715 17s.
From Midsummer 1781 to Midsummer 1782 £597 19s. 4¾d.

If these yearly figures are considered, then clearly the figure of nearly £896 represents the total tolls collected over one year. This view is supported by an entry in one of Edward Sneyd's note-books which states that the toll

Landside view of the 'Endon Tip' showing a standard gauge NSR wagon loaded with limestone from Caldon Low. *J.R. Hollick/Manifold Collection*

Tradition has it that on the first occasion, the flow from the wagon was too sudden and the narrow boat sank. This picture shows a boat that is very unevenly loaded.
J.R. Hollick/Manifold Collection

collected for 'one year on the Caldon Branch from Xmas 78 to do 79 (was) £895 15s. 4¼d.[7] As the account runs from one Christmas to another, in contrast to usual practice of accounting from one Midsummer day (24th June) to the next, Sneyd's note provides the strongest evidence that the Caldon Canal became operational around Christmas 1778. So despite his curious method of estimation, Charles Hadfield's 'guess' at 'a date early in 1779' was quite close to the mark.

Early in 1777 the canal company was still buying land for the canal in the Shelton area, but by 1778 the canal had been carried forward sufficiently to embolden a number of associated projects.[8] Firstly, there was the branch canal to Norton Green built by agreement between John Sparrow, John Hales and Francis Mear. This document (signed on 19th November, 1778) is of great interest as it shows how short branch canals could be built by the consent of landowners without recourse to Parliament. They,

> ... the said parties shall and will as soon as conveniently maybe, at their equal Costs and Charges make a Navigable Cut from the Caldon Navigation near Norton up to Norton Green thro' the Lands of the said Francis Mear called the Paddocks, the Cowhay and the Eyes being in length about four hundred yards and that the said Cut when made shall be the property of them (and their Heirs) in equal Shares as Tenants in Common. And that the satisfaction to be made to the said Francis Mear for the damage done to the said Lands and the yearly value or Rents to be paid for ever hereafter to the said Francis Mear and his Heirs for the Land taken for forming the said Cut shall be left to two indifferent persons One to be chosen by the said John Sparrow and John Hales and the other by the said Francis Mear.[9]

There was also the conversion of the old forge buildings at Consall Forge into a flint mill, confirmed by a lease signed on 2nd March, 1778. This was a joint venture between Thomas Griffin, Francis Leigh and William Bill who had formed a partnership earlier the same year.[10] This was no speculative venture as both Griffin and Bill had earlier converted a mill at Trentham to flint grinding, knowing that the Trent and Mersey Canal would soon be completed and that 'the Pottery trade was (at that time) extremely good'.[11] William Bill was brother-in-law to John and Thomas Gilbert, a member of the management committee of the canal company and resident agent for Earl Gower's Trentham estate. Like many minor eighteenth century entrepreneurs, he was quick to realise the great changes and advantages that the canal age was to bring.[12]

The accounts of the Cheddleton Lime Company begin significantly in December 1778, a further proof that the Caldon Canal opened to traffic during the final month of that year. From 1778 to 1791, the Cheddleton Lime Company bought limestone from the Hemingslow Quarry at Caldon Low, which involved a traffic that depended on the operation of both canal and railway. All this confirms Farey's second date of '1778' and that the canal and railway took two years to build as envisaged in the Act. Edward Sneyd noted the final cost of the total works as £23,560, slightly more than the original estimate accepted in 1776.[13]

References

1. SRO: D554/162.
2. WSL: HM/19.
3. John Farey, *Agriculture and Minerals of Derbyshire*, Vol III, p. 445; and Charles Hadfield, *The Canals of the West Midlands*, p. 299.
4. SRO: D554/91.
5. WSL: HM 37–40.
6. *Abraham Rees's Manufacturing Industry*; N. Cossons (Ed.), Vol. I, p. 407.
7. WSL: HM 37–40.
8. SRO: D(W) 1788/57/2.
9. SRO: D1798/177.
10. SRO: D239/M/1212 and SRO: D554/154.
11. SRO: D554/91.
12. Ross Wordie, *Estate Management in Eighteenth Century England*, p. 47 and WSL: HM 37/19.
13. SRO: D239/M/2139 and WSL: HM/37/37.

Cheddleton Flint Mill used the waters of the River Churnet to power its two undershot waterwheels and the Caldon Canal for transport. *Cheddleton Flint Mill Trust*

Chapter Three
Consolidation

In July 1779 the committee of the Trent and Mersey Canal Company made a survey of the recently commissioned canal, although contemporary records show that a number of the associated works were still to be completed. Josiah Wedgwood took part in this tour of inspection and wrote a delightful account of his excursion:

> I have had my share of the burning heat for some days past, having been on horseback from 9 in the morning 'till 8 at night with little rest or shelter; not more than an hour one of the days. An excursion to Ecton with two of my boys, and at the same time making a survey of the Caldon Canal with Mr (Thomas) Gilbert & others call'd me through these Lybian heats. I contriv'd to sleep at Cotton both the nights I was from home, and a delightful spot it is.[1]

The inadequacies of the system were quickly recognised; and in 1783 the company applied for and obtained a second Act of Parliament (23.Geo.III cap. 33, Royal Assent 17th April, 1783). The main problem was the railway from Froghall to the Caldon Low quarries which in John Farey's words: 'appears to have been set out, before the true principles of this branch of Engineery [sic] was well understood.[2] The line of the railway was altered (see Chapter Nine) and the canal was extended for 530 yds at the Froghall terminal; this involved the construction of the 76 yds-long tunnel and the abandonment of the original loading area.

The Act also allowed for a reservoir on the edge of Stanley Moss (which seems to have been the millpond serving Hercules Mill); and one higher up the same stream towards Bagnall (now called confusingly Stanley Pool). A map published in 1795 clearly marks the smaller and lower reservoir as 'Stanley Pool', and the much larger and slightly higher water as 'Bagnall Reservoir'.[3] The same map locates 'Knipersley Reservoir' described as 'new' in 1783, so it is plain that in the first few years after the Caldon Canal opened the company made great efforts to secure further water supplies.[4] The original 'Stanley Pool' cost the company a modest £99 19s. 7½d. between 1786 and 1789, as presumably only minimal work was required to strengthen the existing dam. The larger 'Bagnall Reservoir' (the modern Stanley Pool) proved much more troublesome. In 1787 and 1788 there were two serious breaches in the dam, such that the construction and repair of the dam (between 1786–1789) cost the massive figure of £4,832 9s.[5] Even later, in 1840, Stanley Pool was further enlarged to its present size when the dam was heightened.[6]

The surviving records from this period reveal that both the Caldon and the Trent and Mersey Canals suffered from a general shortage of water; especially during 1785, 1788–89, 1791 and 1796. William Robinson (Principal Agent and General Superintendent to the company) noted that even in a good year 'many boats had to navigate with half loads in the dry season', adding that in 1785 and 1795 both the canals and reservoirs had 'run dry'.[7]

Expenditure on the Caldon Canal appears to have exceeded receipts until sometime after 1800. The available fragmentary figures[6] reveal the difference between the debt and income during the early years of operation.

NAVIGATION
from the *TRENT* to the *MERSEY*,

At a Meeting of the COMMITTEE of the said NAVIGATION, held at the Crown in Stone, in the County of Stafford, on Thursday the 13th. day of June, 1776.

Present, THOMAS GILBERT Esq; in the Chair.

| John Eld
Edward Salmon } Esqrs.
Richard Moland | The Rev. Dr. *Falconer*,
The Rev. Mr. *Bill*,
Mr. *Wedgwood*, | Mr. *Twemlow*,
Mr. *Phillips*,
Mr. *Hollinshead*, | Mr. *Boyer*,
Mr. *Griffin*,
Mr. *W. Bill*, | Mr. *J. Gilbert*. |

THE Act passed the last Session of Parliament, enabling the Company to make a navigable Canal, from the said *Navigation* on the South side of *Harecastle*, to *Froghall*, and a Railway from thence to or near *Caldon*, by borrowing Money on the Credit of the Tolls thereby granted, (an abstract of which is hereto annexed) was taken into consideration; and it appeared to the *Committee*, to be extremely well calculated for the accommodation of the Country, with the Articles of Lime, and Coal, on very reasonable Terms, and likely to conduce very much to the advantage of the *Proprietors* of the *Trunk Navigation*, not only by increasing their Tonnage, but also, producing a surplus of Tonnage, beyond the Payment of the Interest of the Money to be borrowed, and the necessary expences attending the making and keeping the same in repair.

THE *Committee* also considered the expences which are likely to attend the execution of the said Act, which they apprehend will amount to about 23,000l. besides the Sum of 5000l. which was stipulated (before the passing the Act and which is confirmed by it) to be paid by the owners of some Collieries, for part of the Tonnage upon the Article of Coals only, on the said Railway and a small part of the said intended *Navigation*.

THE *Committee* likewise considered the means which appeared to them most proper and eligible, for procuring the said Sum of 23,000l. and were of opinion, That a Subscription should be opened for a Loan of Money, upon the Credit of the Tolls to arise from the said intended *Navigation* and Railway, with Interest at the rate of 4l. 10s. per Cent, per Annum. which Tolls, upon Calculations made of the probable quantities of Lime-stone, and Coal, to be carried annually upon the said *Navigation* and *Railway*, (without taking into their Calculation a considerable number of other Articles which must necessarily come upon the same) appeared greatly to exceed the amount of the Interest, and other annual expences.

THEY were also of opinion, That a Subscription Paper should be presented, to the most considerable Land Owners who will be benefited by this new *Navigation*, and also to the *Proprietors* of the *Trunk Navigation*, but as those *Proprietors* have already made very large contributions, in respect of their several Shares, it was thought an application to them for the Loan of further Sums, though apparently for their advantage, might be disagreeable or inconvenient, and as many of those *Proprietors*, have besides the Money advanced in respect of their Shares, lent several Sums of Money, on the Credit and Security of the Tolls of that *Navigation*, (which Sums may easily be procured from Persons who have no connection with the *Navigation*, on the Assignment of such Securities) it was thought proper for the ease of such *Proprietors* as are inclined to encourage the execution of the new *Navigation*, that they should be requested to subscribe, such Sums as they shall think fit to transfer from their Securities, to such Persons as will advance the Money thereupon, and to accept new Securities for the like Sums at the same rate of Interest, upon the Tolls to arise from the said new *Navigation* : by which means they will give an effectual support to this intended branch of the *Trunk Navigation*, without advancing any Money, or (as is apprehended) sustaining any loss or diminution of their Property.

THE *Committee*, being fully convinced of the Propriety of this measure, have declared their readiness to exchange their Securities for a considerable part of the Money so advanced by them, on the Terms here submitted.

IN order to collect the Sentiments of the *Proprietors* at large upon this business, so important, and likely to be so beneficial to their property, the *Committee* have thought fit to appoint a *General Assembly*, to be held at the *Crown* in *Stone*, on *Tuesday*, the 23d. day of *July* next, which the several Proprietors are desired to attend in Person, or to signify by a Letter, directed to the *Navigation Office* at *Stone*, the Sum they will be pleased to transfer, or lend, on the Terms aforesaid, upon the Tolls of this new *Navigation*.

By order of the COMMITTEE,

J. SPARROW,

Clerk to the COMPANY.

Courtesy Staffordshire County Record Office

Amount Owing on the Caldon Canal

Year	Amount	Interest paid
1778	£23,560	£1,060 4s.
1783–84	£21,560	£1,078
1786–87	£21,710	£1,085 10s.
1788–89	£21,710	£ 976 19s.
1790–91	£17,710	£ 796 19s.

Receipts on the Caldon Canal

Year	Amount Collected
Christmas 1778–Christmas 1779	£895 15s. 4¼d.
Midsummer 1780–Midsummer 1781	£715 17s. 0d.
Midsummer 1781–Midsummer 1782	£597 19s. 4¾d.

The falling off in receipts between 1780 and 1782 may be a further indicator of the problems being experienced with the first Caldon Low railway, which were not fully rectified until 1785 when the realignment and improvement of the line was largely completed. The first limekilns at Froghall Wharf went into use in June 1786 and cost the company £312 12s. 4d. They still stand to the north of Froghall Basin, adjacent to the modern picnic area. The relatively high levels of expenditure might well have caused the management committee to question the wisdom of the whole Caldon Canal project, but in fact it was already proving to be a priceless asset to them. As a branch canal carrying traffic and raising tolls it was definitely a long term investment, but as Thomas Sparrow (Company Clerk) noted in his report for 1787:

> The Caldon branch has greatly contributed to the assistance of this NAVIGATION, not only as the vehicle of the waters from ... Reservoirs, but also of others, necessary to its support, into the summit at Harecastle, from whence the numerous Locks to the Trent, and to the Mersey, are filled and supplied.

During the financial years 1786–87, the Trent and Mersey Canal Company's turnover was £31,239 'which greatly exceeded the produce of any proceeding year'.[8] It is almost certain that the Trent and Mersey Canal would have been inoperable without the water supply delivered by the Caldon Canal.

As the traffic on the main line increased, so did the demand for water. A further reservoir in Rudyard Vale was completed in 1799, but water from this source could not reach the Caldon Canal until the Leek Canal opened in 1801[9] (see also Chapter Seven). Even with this new supply it was still not enough, especially when the Uttoxeter Canal opened in 1811. During 1820 and 1821, the company was consulting John Rennie about the need for a second tunnel through Harecastle Hill, so they took the opportunity of seeking his advice on improvements to the Rudyard and Knypersley Reservoirs. The company were proposing a second reservoir at Knypersley but Rennie felt that a general improvement to existing supplies would be more effective. Before anything could be settled, John Rennie died in October 1821. Not until 17th June, 1823 did the company obtain the parliamentary

George Tomlinson delivering coal slack to Cheddleton Paper Mills, pre-1951. His skewbald pony was well known along the canal.   *Caldon Canal Society*

One of the best known boats ever to navigate the Caldon Canal was *Perpetual* owned by William Podmore and Sons of Consall Mills. This boat was first registered to the Anderton Carrying Company as *Brussels*.   *Caldon Canal Society*

powers to build the new reservoir (4 Geo.IV cap. 87). Meanwhile they had consulted Thomas Telford about both the new tunnel and reservoir.[10] In both these tasks Telford was aided by James Potter in the role of Resident Engineer, possibly the son of a namesake who had worked with Rennie on the Rudyard Reservoir.[11]

The new reservoir was to prove most troublesome. There were continual problems with leakage through the discharge well and the dam wall. Such were the apparent dangers that the owners of land situated below the dam made strong representations to a special meeting of the canal company's management committee. In July 1828 the reservoir was emptied as a precautionary measure and the committee sought further advice from George Hamilton and James Trubshaw.[12] Trubshaw had already been consulted by the canal company (and in particular Josiah Wedgwood II) about various aspects of canal engineering including the Harecastle Tunnel. He had a long association with the canal company and was to design the last of the Caldon Low railways. However, he never appears to have visited Knypersley; and it was either his brother John, or nephew John who was summoned there. John Trubshaw had been sent for several times during the insertion of the pipes to watch the method of work. This caused Potter to complain to Telford that 'this is of course not only an insult to myself, but also to you'.[13]

Telford must have found this 'supervision' by a member of the Trubshaw family irksome, for at the time James Trubshaw was building the Grosvenor Bridge at Chester, which Telford had declared 'inadvisable' because of its 200 ft span. Potter left the company's employ in disgust, having received no paid employment with the company since the completion of the second Harecastle Tunnel. Telford received a further approach from William Vaughan (the company Secretary) in September 1830, requesting further advice as the leakage problems were as bad as ever.[14] Nothing further is known of this unhappy affair and the 1840 tithe map shows both the 'old reservoir' (now known as the Serpentine) and the 'new reservoir'.[15]

A survey undertaken in 1795 reveals that there were some 41 'local' boats operating on the Caldon Canal. Nine of these were owned by John Sparrow & Company who used them to transport coal from the Cockshead Colliery at Norton. John Rennie noted that this coal reached markets up to 40 miles away, although most customers were to be found within 10 miles of the colliery.[16] The Caldon Lime Company at Cheddleton operated seven boats, and Thomas Griffin & Company, of Consall Mills, a single boat carrying flint to the mill. All the other boats were operated by their owners who lived close to the canal, but other boats must have come from outside the area to collect limestone and coal. Some idea of the traffic in limestone can be deduced from the figure of 40,000 tons reported to have been carried on the branch in 1797.[17] This probably represents nearly 2,000 boat trips and an income of around £2,000 in tolls.

The Caldon Lime Company was in fact the same as the Cheddleton Lime Company, the names being used in an interchangeable fashion. The partnership was made up of John Gilbert (Senior), John Gilbert (Junior), Sampson Whieldon, Richard Hill and George Smith. All of them were involved in

Cheddleton Wharf in 1905 showing a fully loaded Brunner-Mond boat. In the foreground there is an interesting example of a canal ice-breaker, tied up alongside the former boatyard. *Caldon Canal Society*

Cheddleton Wharf, c.1899; the piles of bricks were known to be for the construction of the County Mental Hospital. *Caldon Canal Society*

quarrying at Caldon Low, hence the name the Caldon Lime Company; and the centre for their limeburning operation was at Cheddleton, therefore the Cheddleton Lime Company. From 1778 they operated the limekilns at a point just beyond the modern Flintlock Restaurant. They also operated limekilns at Horsebridge (Denford), and possibly the two limekilns which stood on the site now occupied by the Boat Inn at Cheddleton.[18] Coal was obtained from the nearby Shafferlong Coalfield, and payments for consignments were made to the Reverend Edward Powys who had contracted to supply John Gilbert and his partners. The company also operated a dockyard at Cheddleton, just to the east of the road bridge where they built their own narrow boats.

The kilns at Cheddleton were the cause of great nuisance to the local inhabitants, who were partially pacified by yearly payments of 10s. 6d. The Cheddleton Company ceased trading in 1834, but around 1850 Elijah and Thomas Heath were still burning lime at Cheddleton.[19] Limekilns are known to have existed at Basford Bridge, Denford, Stanley Moss, Norton Green, Leek and Consall Forge. Many more existed and some have left a reminder in the form of a place name, such as Limekiln Bank where the A52 crosses the canal between Bucknall and Hanley.

Caldon limestone was conveyed for considerable distances and used for manuring the land, in the building trade and as a flux in iron smelting. Following the completion of the Trent and Mersey Canal, John Gilbert and his son John, soon established a steady seasonal trade in supplying broken limestone to the various kilns along the local canal system. They supplied their own kilns at Cheddleton and Denford as part of the partnership arrangements within the Cheddleton Lime Company, but as early as 1781 they were making regular deliveries to the Etruria and Longport kilns. John Gilbert (Junior) extended this interest when he established limekilns and a coalyard at Stonefield (near Stone) in 1796. Burnt lime was reaching Acton Bridge (in Cheshire) before 1800, having been 'brought by the Staffordshire Canal, in iron boats, from the neighbourhood of Leek'.[20]

This trade may have been even more widespread as the Forebridge kilns at Stafford were burning 'Froghall stone' as well as Dudley limestone by 1812. The younger John Gilbert was able to maximise the return from his carrying operations between Froghall and Kidsgrove after 1806, when he 'contracted with the Lime burners for all (slack) I now get'. This is revealed in a letter to Josiah Wedgwood II, written in June of that year; but the seasonal nature of the trade is underlined by his comment that 'in about two months this trade will decrease'. John Farey observed this trade and noted 'I saw the Caldon and Froghall Limeworks in 1808 [and] the coals used thereat, were brought 22 miles along the canal, from Mr Gilbert's Kidcrew (Kidsgrove) collieries'.

As soon as the canal reached the Norton area, John Sparrow formed a partnership with a number of local potters to launch the Cockshead Colliery Company. Under the agreement signed in 1778, Sparrow built this short branch canal from a point near Heakley Hall Farm to Norton Green. The main traffic was in coal, but the branch also carried broken limestone to the colliery company's kiln which stood near the main road at Norton Green. Just before the terminus of the canal was the main coal winding shaft where a Boulton and Watt engine was employed from 1793. The colliery was originally drained by a water engine, but this was replaced in 1792 by another Boulton and Watt engine that stood a little to the north of Engine Lock.[21] When John Rennie examined this engine in 1798, he noted that it worked at the rate of ten strokes a minute, each stroke raising 110 gallons of water which passed straight into the canal. Such a mutually advantageous arrangement could not have failed to have pleased the canal company. The colliery was being operated by six Longton pottery manufactureres in 1836, but by 1847 it was proposed to sell it by auction and thereafter there is no evidence that it ever worked again.[22]. Other collieries were developed around Norton-in-the-Moors and Downfield Side, but due to the steeply sloping terrain they were linked to the canal by tramroads.[23]

Josiah Wedgwood suggested a further branch from the Caldon Canal (near Milton) to the Whitfield Collieries, proposing that the mines be worked in the same way as the Duke of Bridgewater's collieries and those in Harecastle Hill. In both these cases coal was carried from the working face to the outside world by subterranean canals. Some sort of rudimentary survey was made and the cost estimated at £1,300 per mile, but his proposal did not receive much support from his fellow proprietors.[24] Possibly it was the remembrance of this design that prompted a tramroad scheme in 1800. This set out a plan for a line from Foxley (near Milton) past Whitfield to Knypersley, where there were a number of coal and ironstone mines.[25] A further survey made in 1812 proposed a branch from Milton 'to pass by a Tunnel under the Grand Ridge (through coal measures), into the valley of the Dane near Congleton'. This would have run under Biddulph and then gone around Congleton to Macclesfield, to effect a junction with the Duke of Bridgewater's canal at Sale Moor. The prospect of a rival supply of coal would not have filled the Duke's trustees with much glee, so not surprisingly it was never more than an outline proposal of the sort that abounded during the 'Canal mania'.[26]

In the area between Consall Forge and Froghall a number of collieries were active during the same period. Foxtwood Colliery was owned by the Duke of Devonshire who used it to supply his smelters at Whiston Copper Works. Across the valley at Hazlecross, the Duke had another colliery which was drained by the impressive 1¼ mile long sound known as the 'Duke's Level'. Most of the coal was intended for the local market, but in 1794 there was a definite plan to develop an outward trade in coal. In that year 'Mr Cross, the Navigation Agent and his son with Mr Allin and some others' were involved 'in setting out the proposed Railway from the Canal to Kingsley Colliery'.[27] Like so many similar projects it was allowed to lapse.

Flint milling provided another important and enduring trade on the Caldon Canal. Both mills at Cheddleton were grinding flint by 1815 and it is certain that the process had been established there long before this date. These mills were operated by John Leigh between 1815 and 1840, which accounts for the presence of the tramroad system there using rails of the type employed on the North Stafford Railway of 1815. At Consall Forge the flint mills were erected in 1778 on the site of one of the old ironworks. They were in the possession of John Leigh by 1811 and he developed them into their

Consall Forge, where the Caldon Canal leaves the River Churnet, as it flows under the bridge (*to the right*). The narrow boat is one of those that carried limestone to South Staffordshire. *Author's Collection*

Consall Forge in 1910. The stop-gates prevented the floodwaters of the River Churnet from entering the canal. *Author's Collection*

present basic shape. The surviving mill buildings were called the 'upper mills' but nearby can be seen the remains of the 'lower mills'. These became derelict when the Churnet Valley Railway was built across the millpond, but despite years of decay one still retains remnants of its oak gearing. John Leigh was declared bankrupt in 1841; and the mills were offered for sale with the enticement that annual profits were said to be between £3,000– 4,000.[28] Near to the Consall Mills may be found the remains of Crowgutter Mill, which was probably a purpose built flint mill known to have been in production by 1811. At Froghall, Cupola Mill was grinding flint by 1812 and like the mills at Cheddleton it had a tramroad link with the canal.[29]

The late Professor S.H. Beaver demonstrated that the building of the Trent and Mersey Canals did little to encourage potters to follow the example of Josiah Wedgwood and move to canalside locations. This can be explained by a simple economic fact regarding the proportions of coal and clay that were used in pottery factories. At least six times as much coal as clay was needed to make a given quantity of ware; so it was in the manufacturer's best interests to remain in the old production centres on the Black Band Coal Measures. This did not hold true for Caldon Canal, especially below Hanley where the canal passed over these same coal measures.[30] A number of pottery factories grew up in this 'corridor', most notably the Eagle Pottery and that belonging to John Ridgway at Caldon Place, Shelton. Simeon Shaw in his *History of the Staffordshire Potteries* described the advantages of this site in 1829: 'opportunity is enjoyed for receiving coals and all materials, and for forwarding all packages, by canal conveyances'. Numerous small collieries sprang up to serve these works, including one at Joiner's Square with its own short tramroad to the Caldon Canal.[31]

In the same general area there were a number of other small factories. Henry Fourdrinier established a paper mill at Ivy House in 1827, supplying tissue paper for use in the pottery industry. He effectively put the rival Cheddleton Paper Mill (established in 1797) out of business, then bought it and built a new mill on the site.[32] Some important foundries were also to be found in this area of Hanley, including one erected by a local engineer, William Heath in 1809. He worked closely with Richard Trevithick and made a sustained if profitless attempt to introduce high pressure steam engines to North Staffordshire.[33] Close to the canal at Ford Green there was a curious concern called the 'Ford Green Steam Scrap Forge'. Little is known about this establishment, other than it operated from 1802 to 1818 and received consignments of scrap by boat.[34]

At the end of the 18th century, the canal company was considering building a branch canal from a point above the locks at Etruria to serve Shelton and Hanley. They consulted John Rennie who examined the ground in August 1797 and then submitted two alternative plans. One involved the construction of four locks and a steam engine to supply the highest level with water; and the other proposal was to use a novel caisson lock. Rennie was particularly interested in the caisson lock invented by Robert Weldon from Lichfield. Weldon appears to have enjoyed the patronage of Thomas Gilbert, who was M.P. for Lichfield until 1794. In June of that year, Gilbert's kinsman John Ward (who was involved in the planning of the Kennet and Avon Canal) wrote:

> I saw Mr Gilbert at Cotton on Tuesday night. He was very earnest in recommending it to our committee to send Rennie into Shropshire to see a cassoon which is calculated to raise and sink boats from one level to another without waste of water. Weldon is the patentee and the cassoon is at Wrockwardine, near Lilleshall in Shropshire.[35]

At the time Thomas Gilbert was 74 years of age but still passionately interested in promoting canals and new technology. Unfortunately, Weldon's caisson lock experienced problems caused by geological difficulties when tried at Coombe Hay, near Bath; so Rennie decided by 1798 that 'no satisfactory trial' had been carried out.[36] He then came up with a third alternative that of building a tramroad from Etruria to Hanley with branches to local collieries and factories. This was accepted by the company who included it in an Act of Parliament (42.Geo.III cap. 25, Royal Assent 15th April, 1802) and the railway was built between 1803 and 1804.

References

1. K.E. Farrer, loc. cit., pp. 499–500.
2. *Abraham Rees's Manufacturing Industry*; N. Cossons (Ed.), Vol. I, p. 407.
3. J. Aikin, A *Description of the Country from Thirty to Forty Miles Round Manchester*, (1795), p. 116.
4. J. Kennedy (Ed.), *Biddulph: A Local History*, (1980), p. 52.
5. WSL: HM/37/19.
6. Robert Speake, *The Old Road to Endon*, (1974), p. 150.
7. SRO: D593/V/3/29.
8. WSL: HM/37/19.
9. John Farey, op. cit., and John Rennie's Notebook, No. 26.
10. L.T.C. Rolt, *Thomas Telford*, (1958), pp. 162–168.
11. John Farey, op. cit., p. 442.
12. L.T.C. Rolt, op. cit., p. 167.
13. Anne Bayliss, *The Life and Works of James Trubshaw*, (1978), pp. 67–8.
14. L.T.C. Rolt, op. cit., p. 168.
15. SRO: Parish of Biddulph Tithe map.
16. SRO: QR/Ub and John Rennie's Notebook, No. 26.
17. SRO: D593/V/3/29 and D239/M/2138–2143.
18. *Evening Sentinel*, 6th August, 1983.
19. SRO: D239/M/2146 and Robert Milner (Ed.), *Cheddleton*, (1983), pp. 105–107.
20. William Marshall, *The Review and Abstract of the County Reports to the Board of Agriculture From the several Agricultural Departments of England: Western Division* (1818), p. 141.
21. Peter Lead and John Robey, 'Steam Power in North Staffordshire, 1750–1850', *JSIAS*, No. 9 (1980), pp. 17–18.
22. SRO: D239/M/3725 and *Staffordshire Advertiser*, 18th September, 1847.
23. First Edition O.S. (1834).
24. John Thomas, *Rise of Staffordshire Potteries*, (1971), p. 69.
25. SRO: Q/RUm/28.

26 John Farey, op. cit., p. 440.
27 Herbert Chester, *Cheadle Coal Town*, (1981), p. 48; additional information from Dr John Robey.
28 Robert Copeland, *A short history of . . . Cheddleton Flint Mill*, (1972), p. 22 and SRO: D1176/B/3/11.
29 *Staffordshire Advertiser*, 21st September, 1811.
30 S.H. Beaver, 'The Potteries: A Study in the Evolution of a Cultural Landscape', *Trans. Inst. British Geographers, no. 34* (1964), p. 14.
31 Thomas Hargreaves, *Map of the Staffordshire Potteries and Newcastle*, (1832), copy in Hanley Library.
32 John Thomas, op. cit., p. 60.
33 Peter Lead and Hugh Torrens, 'Richard Trevithick, The Heath Family and the North Staffordshire Connection', *Jn. Trevithick Society*, No. 10, (1983), pp. 59–69.
34 *Staffordshire Advertiser*, 29th May, 1802 and 6th June, 1818.
35 Michael Corfield, 'John Ward and the Kennet and Avon Canal, Part 2', *Jn. Bristol Industrial Archaeology Society*, no. 15, (1983), p. 23.
36 I am most grateful to Dr Hugh Torrens, Department of Geology, University of Keele for this information on John Rennie's work.

The boat *Farmers Friend* seen loaded near Consall Forge before the First World War. This photograph conveys the sense of joy at travelling through a sylvan glade.
Caldon Canal Society

Chapter Four
A Period of Prosperity

Faced by the fierce competition from rival quarry owners like those at Crich, the Trent and Mersey Canal Company realised that they had to increase production from the Caldon Low quarries if they were to survive in the limestone trade. One way was to improve the canal and the railway, but another was to take over quarrying operations themselves.[1] In 1836 a further Act of Parliament (1 Will.IV cap. 55) gave the company authority to widen and straighten the canal between Oakmeadow Lock and Flint Mill Lock. This was in the main, the section of the canal which occupied the bed and course of the River Churnet as it went through the gorge near Consall Forge. By 1841 they had taken over quarrying at Caldon Low and removed the bottle-neck around Denford and Hazelhurst. It was part of a general scheme of improvement which included a new railway from Froghall to Caldon Low; so that when the North Staffordshire Railway Company bought the canal company in 1847 they found the programme virtually complete.

The railway company had no intention of allowing the traffic on the canal to decline, although the construction of the railway spur from Froghall Junction to Froghall Wharf (sometime between 1857–1879) did alter the traffic flow pattern.[2] After this, the bulk of the limestone destined for South Staffordshire went by railway down the Churnet Valley Line, whilst the north-bound traffic was generally divided fairly evenly between the canal and the railway.[3] Initially, the railway company found that the limestone business was highly competitive, so they sought a reduction in the royalties payable to the quarry owners. They cited quarries in South Wales and South Staffordshire, as well as those at Bugsworth and Clay Cross. As a remedy they asked the quarry owners to take 1d. instead of 2d. a ton, plus an increase from 21 cwt to 24 cwt per ton. The precise response from the quarry owners has not been recorded, but some unknown clerk endorsed the relevant document in laconic fashion 'not accepted'.[4]

Fortune did smile on the North Staffordshire Railway Company as owners of the Caldon Canal within a few years. Sometime in 1852, William Bishop rediscovered the band of ore known as Froghall haematite whilst prospecting for coal near Crowgutter Mill. He did not live long enough to benefit from his find, but others were very interested in its iron content and its high proportion of calcium oxide. In general the iron content averaged out at approximately 50 per cent, but it generally contained an average of 20 per cent lime in some form or another. This high lime content made it easy to smelt and it was in great demand with the South Staffordshire ironmasters who used it to help in the smelting of the poorer quality ores.[5]

The ore occurs in an area roughly elliptical in shape, extending from Consall New Hall to the Mosey Moor Valley and Ipstones Park. Fortunately, for the mine operators and the railway company (as canal owners and operators), the Caldon Canal and the Churnet Valley Line intersected this ore-field. Commercial production appears to have begun in 1854, when workings were opened near Consall Mills and in Mosey Moor Wood. It rapidly spread and during the prosperous years 1856–1869, an average of 415,964 tons were despatched per annum. About half went by canal (from

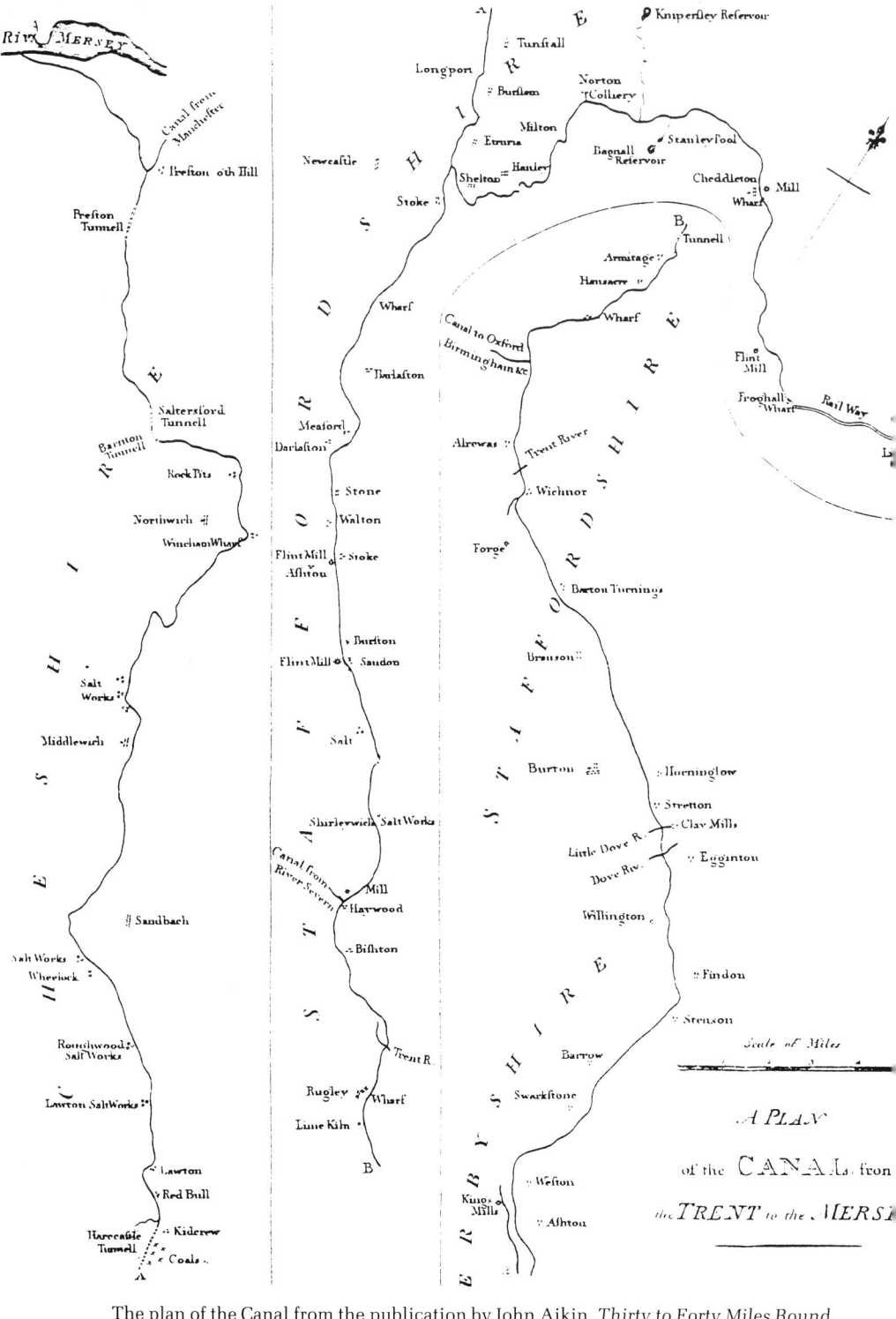

The plan of the Canal from the publication by John Aikin, *Thirty to Forty Miles Round Manchester*, published 1795.

the dozen or so wharves between Consall Forge and Froghall) and the rest left on the railway. Assuming some 200,000 tons were transported by canal with an average boat load of 22 tons; this gives a yearly passage of nearly 10,000 ironstone boats. Simple arithmetic confirms that the figure of about 30 ironstone boats a day as remembered by old folk is relatively accurate. Between 1869–1881 production fell to a yearly average of 42,280 tons; so it can be assumed that less than 5 boats may have been involved in the daily carriage of ironstone during this period.[6]

The Census Returns for 1851 and 1861 also confirm these developments. No ironstone miners appear in the 1851 returns, but 10 years later there are numerous references to them. The 1861 return also records 15 boats engaged in the ironstone traffic, carrying an average of 22 tons and all hailing from Birmingham and the Black Country. A further six boats are listed, although it is impossible to determine whether they were carrying ironstone or broken limestone. Five of the crews had made the journey from the Black Country, but James Clowes and his family were local folk from Stockton Brook.[7]

Further evidence for the scale of these operations is provided by the numerous old workings, abandoned inclines and canalside wharves that can still be seen in the area. One of these inclines served the last of the ironstone mines, the so-called Cherry Eye Mine, whose name is perpetuated by the unique bridge between Consall Mills and Froghall. Towards the end of its useful life, the mine produced a very red ironstone that was used mainly for paint making. It was carried to Froghall by boat and crushed in the mill by the station. The mine finally closed in 1923 when the millowner found that he could obtain Spanish haematite far cheaper than it could be produced locally.[8]

Cherryeye Bridge in 1920. This unusual bridge reflects the architectural taste of a local landowner and stands in complete contrast to the more conventional styles found elsewhere on the canal. *Author's Collection*

A certain William Eli Bowers played a central part in the development of the ore-field, but he also operated the limekilns at Froghall Wharf from around 1851. As well as this he was a local coalmaster who leased the Woodhead Colliery and it seems likely that slack from that colliery was used in the limekilns.[9] By 1912 the business at Froghall Wharf was known as Bowers and Thorley; and their boat *Farmers' Friend* was well known along the Caldon. One photograph shows it scrubbed clean for a Sunday outing. Limeburning continued at Froghall Wharf into the 1930s, but by this time the limestone was brought down from Caldon Low by lorry.[10] Broken lime was bought in considerable quantities by the Cheshire firm of Brunner-Mond (now I.C.I.), who had large alkali works at Middlewich and Northwich. A fleet of about 10 boats operated between these sites and Froghall. The trade appears to have started in the 1880s and the company's boats commonly figure in photographs taken between 1900 and 1920.

References

1   SRO:D239/M/3925.
2   Map by J. Boot of 'the Minerals of Kingsley School Lands in the parish of Checkley', (1857); and first edition, Ordnance Survey — main railways (but not Caldon Low tramway) updated to 1879.
3   Information from the late Herbert Chester.
4   SRO: D554/84.
5   Herbert Chester, *The Iron Valley*, (1979), pp. 76–77.
6   Information in this paragraph came from the late Herbert Chester.
7   Information from Robert Speake.
8   Herbert Chester, op. cit., p. 100.
9   R.A. Lewis, *Directories of Cheadle and District*, (1973), various entries.
10 Information from C.M. Beardmore.

Perpetual was known locally as a 'buttermilk boat' as she sometimes carried flint in a slop condition from Crowgutter Mill.   *Henry Podmore*

Chapter Five
Decline

The Brunner-Mond contract was cancelled in 1920 and this coupled with the increased use of the standard gauge railway from Leekbrook to the Caldon Low quarries made the maintenance of the last tramway uneconomic. There had been during World War I an almost insatiable demand for limestone, so that in 1917 the railway company installed new crushers at Caldon Low and a new mechanical stone chute and hopper at the Endon canal basin. The designer was Thomas F. Coleman and the idea was to transfer crushed stone from railway wagons into canal boats. The wagons were clamped to the rails and rotated to allow the stone to fall into the boats in a regulated flow, so as to avoid damaging the boat. Transhipment was still being carried on at the basin in 1928, but ceased within a few years.[1]

Coal remained an important traffic on the canal, especially from the collieries at Norton. The Norton Ironworks (near Ford Green) were established by Robert Heath and in production by 1866.[2] He also operated Norton Colliery as part of a fully integrated works, the whole of which was served chiefly by the Biddulph Valley line of the North Staffordshire Railway. A short branch canal was also built from Foxley, which brought limestone and at one time Froghall ironstone to the works. This branch built sometime around 1866 is often confused with the Norton Green branch, built much earlier for the Cockshead Colliery Company. A regular traffic in coal continued between Foxley and Leek until 1934.[3] Elsewhere regular deliveries of slack were made to the Cheddleton Paper Mills by Mr George Tomkinson. His skewbald pony was a familiar sight between Endon and Cheddleton until Mr Tomkinson's retirement in 1951.[4]

Potters' materials had remained an important traffic on the Caldon Canal until 1950, when Podmore's replaced their narrow boat *Perpetual* with lorries using the new road down to Consall Mills. Previously, this boat had been used to carry ground materials from both Crowgutter and Consall Mills to the company's other mill at Shelton.[5] George Mellor and Company operated two boats carrying coal between Cockshute Sidings and their Etruria Vale Mill until sometime after 1949.[6] Further up the canal, J. and G. Meakin of the Eagle Pottery had a small fleet of four narrow boats which brought potters' materials from Weston Point Docks.[7] Most of their export traffic was carried by boat until 1930, but they did not sell the last of their boats until 1953.[8] A most interesting photograph was taken in the early 1920s and shows three of this company's boats drawn up side by side behind the Eagle Pottery. Planking had been placed across the boats to construct a pontoon style bridge. Astride this can be seen a massive boiler, which had proved too large to pass through the factory entrance, so it was manoeuvered in through 'the back door'.

During 1955 part of the canal was dredged in an abortive attempt to encourage a traffic in coal down to Froghall. Thomas Bolton and Sons' canalside works had received slack for the steam generating plant by boat

Consall Flint Mills, 1923. The abandoned lock (*to the left of centre*) and the small tramroad system on the left bank are worthy of note. *Author's Collection*

A delightful photograph showing a narrow boat being towed back towards the winding hole at Consall Forge, *c*.1900. *P. Wilson*

The tramway bridge which crossed over railway, river and navigation to deliver ironstone mined on Kingsley Banks to a canalside wharf. The photograph was taken c.1880 and the one-legged man was William Sargeant, agent to the Woodhead Mining Company.   *George Short*

An empty narrow boat near Far Kingsley Banks, 1905.   *The late Olive A. Dale*

until World War II; so this appears to have been an attempt to encourage them to do so again.[9] At one time, Boltons owned and operated four narrow boats: *Beatrice; Havelock, Lily of the Lake* and *Nora*. All had been broken up by 1953, except for *Beatrice* which was a former Brunner-Mond boat.[10] The decline of the canal seemed irreversible and in 1961 a notice appeared at Etruria announcing the closure of the canal. Thankfully, it was never fully implemented.[11]

References

1. Charles Hadfield, op. cit., p. 230; Robert Speake, op. cit., p. 154; and Peter Lead, *Trent and Mersey Canal*, captions 87–88.
2. Joseph Kennedy, op. cit., p. 82.
3. Charles Hadfield, op. cit., p.230.
4. Robert Speake, op. cit., p. 154.
5. Information from Henry L. Podmore.
6. HRL: S/138/6.
7. Information from Mr R. Fletcher.
8. HRL: S/138/6.
9. Information from Mr V.B. Hysel.
10. HRL: S/138/6.
11. SCC, *The Caldon Canal, 1779–1974*, (Souvenir Brochure and Programme), p. 16.

A busy scene with breaking and loading limestone into boats moored in what had been the entrance to the top lock of the Uttoxeter Canal. B.H. Snow

Chapter Six
Restoration and New Life

A curious fact is that the Caldon Canal was never formally closed to navigation, despite the notice that appeared at Etruria in 1961. The main reason for this was that the canal was still needed to supply water to the Trent and Mersey Canal, but it was in a terrible state. One writer catalogued the many problems brought on by years of neglect:

> Lock gates had fallen into disrepair, and lock chambers decayed; long stretches were silted-up and reed-infested; towpaths and hedges were overgrown; and in several places seepage was occurring, due to slipping and subsidence of the banks. Near Froghall the problem of slipping was so bad that a length of the canal had to be piped; whilst the lining of the nearby Froghall tunnel was beginning to collapse. Scarcely could the future of a canal have seemed more bleak.[1]

To many people it seemed that the Caldon Canal would suffer the same fate as the nearby Newcastle-under-Lyme Canal, which had been systematically abandoned and infilled. Hopes rose when the National Trust approached British Waterways Board with a view to taking over the canal, but after 18 months it became apparent that more positive action was needed. A meeting at Leek in February 1963 put forward a number of schemes to publicise the plight of the canal and all those present determined to reverse the trend towards complete dereliction. Members of the Stoke Boat Club (whose headquarters were on the only surviving portion of the Newcastle Canal) had been working to polarise public support, a task soon taken over by a special Caldon Canal Committee. This committee became the Caldon Canal Society, which was formed on the 4th April, 1963; and soon monthly working parties were instituted to prevent the canal declining still further.[2]

Initially, these working parties concentrated their efforts on the lower reaches of the canal and most of the projects were land-based. Work on the water channel itself became possible as liaison with British Waterways Board developed, so that parties began to work on the more remote parts of the canal. The Chairman of the Caldon Canal Society, Gordon Myatt described how work progressed during this period:

> The Society had been fortunate in having the wholehearted support of the Stoke-on-Trent Boat Club whose members have provided the expertise and enthusiasm needed to keep the work going in a purposeful manner. Hedge-cutting, towpath clearing and sedge removal, together with the clearance of lock chambers, have constituted the major part of the work and have helped considerably to improve the water channel between the summit at Hazelhurst and Etruria. Much ingenuity has been shown during these working party sessions and they have involved a considerable amount of effort.
>
> The whole appearance of the canal has been improved greatly and it has produced practical results as more casual walkers are visiting the area. The original Committee proved most successful in bringing together all users of the waterway, including boat owners, canoeists, ramblers, fishermen and field club and natural history enthusiasts and all members have worked as a team with the single purpose of maintaining the Caldon Canal from Etruria to Froghall.

Thomas Bolton and Sons used their 'flotilla' to carry coal slack for the steam generating plant at Froghall. Here an empty boat is being towed back to the winding hole in the early 1920s. *Caldon Canal Society*

Bolton's took delivery of *Beatrice* in 1916 and this photograph records her arrival at the Froghall Works. This boat was described as being 'sunk in Froghall Basin' in 1964. *Author's Collection*

Bolton's Works in 1905, when construction work was still underway at Froghall. The smoke is from the limekilns at Froghall Wharf. *The late Olive A. Dale*

Workmen unloading clay for the repair of a breach at Froghall, c.1910. It is interesting to note that the spades and wheel-barrows are identical to those used by the original 'Navvies'. *J.R. Hollick/Manifold Collection*

Despite the sometimes Herculean labours of the volunteers, the rate of progress was unavoidably slow. The Society's resources were slight and British Waterways Board only had enough money to maintain the standard of the water channel. The situation was confirmed when the canal was listed as a 'remainder waterway' and not a 'cruising waterway' under the 1968 Transport Act.

The future seemed bleak, but undaunted the Society appealed to the local authorities for financial assistance; and this resulted in an agreement between British Waterways Board, Staffordshire County Council and Stoke-on-Trent City Council to restore the canal to full navigational use. The work was originally planned to spread over five years, but due to the state of the canal it was condensed to a two year programme. This was inaugurated on 22nd August, 1972, when a new top gate was lowered into place at Engine Lock. British Waterways Board carried out the major repairs to the navigational channel. This involved dredging over 68,000 tonnes of silt and debris from the canal; the complete rebuilding of two lock chambers; and the replacement of nine sets of top and bottom lock gates. In addition, remedial work was needed on various locks, bye-weirs and other associated structures. Extensive repairs were carried out to the lining of the Froghall tunnel and the dammed and piped section of canal was reinstated. The Caldon Canal Society made a major contribution by clearing and surfacing lengths of the towing path, which saved an estimated £10,000.

Once all the vital work was completed, the canal was reopened to traffic on 28th September, 1974. The widow of the former Chairman of Staffordshire County Council, Mrs G. Oxford, and the Lord Mayor of Stoke-on-Trent, Mr Harry Smallwood, in the presence of the Chairman of British Waterways Board, declared the canal to be once again open to navigation. After cutting the tape and unveiling a commemorative plaque at Cheddleton Top Lock, the official party and guests embarked on a 'flotilla of boats' and cruised down to Consall Forge for a buffet lunch.[3] There was something paradoxical about the reopening as the Caldon had never been formally opened back in 1778, but to most boating enthusiasts it did not matter as it was the realisation of a dream.

Despite the changed role of inland waterways many people still see commercial traffic as being the true mark of a living canal. Johnson Brothers (part of the earthenware division of the Wedgwood Group) make use of the Caldon Canal to carry finished ware between their Hanley factory and the associated packing warehouse at Milton. Two specially built narrow boats *Milton Maid* and *Milton Queen* were introduced in 1967 and 1973 respectively. They were built in a disused warehouse under the direction of the company's former engineering executive, Mr Geoffrey Bird. Each boat is about 60 ft long, by 7 ft wide and capable of carrying 20 tons of earthenware.

The savings made by this innovative arrangement arise from the fact that each boat costs one third of the price of a specially designed lorry trailer and is capable of carrying three times the load. Transporting ware over this short distance by canal reduced costs by nearly 50 per cent and the elimination of road hazards cut down the number of breakages by over two-third. Occasional operational set-backs have been experienced; between 1967 and

The Froghall Tunnel was not part of the original canal works as opened in 1778, but formed part of a 540 yard extension opened seven years later. *Author's Collection*

The narrow boat *Edward* entering the north-east portal of the Froghall Tunnel in 1902. *Author's Collection*

1978, the *Milton Maid* turned turtle three times. In November 1976, earthenware worth £3,000 was dumped into the canal, but most of it was retrieved intact and breakages only ran to £200.[4]

A further boat was added to this small fleet in 1978, when the *Milton Princess* was commissioned, so now this small fleet of boats carries some 7000 tonnes of tableware each year. An unsuccessful attempt to reintroduce a trade in coal was made in 1976, when Colin and Pat Walker brought a 16 ton load up as far as Cheddleton. They were aiming at the domestic market, but found that most folk were loathe to leave their regular coal merchants.[5]

After many years of dereliction the wharf at Froghall took on a new lease of life in 1979, when Froghall Wharf Passenger Service was established by Jacki and Bill Young. The main aim of this enterprise was to run public and private charter trips in the butty *Birdswood*, but the old warehouse has also been sympathetically renovated as the Wharf Restaurant. This coincided with a limited redevelopment of the wharf by British Waterways Board and Staffordshire County Council, to provide picnic areas and toilets for visitors.[6] Today the wharf area has an air of serenity, in complete contrast to the hectic activity that surrounded it in the years before 1920.

Just as it did during its commercial heyday, the canal needs constant maintenance, repair and improvement. This becomes glaringly obvious when a major breach occurs like the one which appeared near Froghall on 24th August, 1979. Some five million gallons of water disappeared from a 2½ mile length between Froghall Wharf and the Flint Mills at Consall.[7] This particular area has always presented problems due to geological faulting, numerous springs and a predisposition to landslips. This catalogue of problems is not new and we have clear evidence that this has been a constant problem. There is the abandoned lock near Consall Mills, and Froghall tunnel itself which averted the need to construct an extensive embankment around a steep sided spur. Records from the mid-19th century relate the problems and expense associated with this length of the canal and so British Waterways Board's remedial work is part of a continuous historical programme.[8]

When the campaign was begun to restore the canal a suggestion was made that Froghall Wharf should be converted into a memorial to James Brindley.[9] This would not have been very appropriate as James Brindley had little to do with the Caldon Canal project. More recently work is going ahead on a statue of Brindley to be erected at the junction of the Trent and Mersey and Caldon Canals.[10] The choice of the site would doubtless have made Josiah Wedgwood chuckle as he had considerable trouble persuading Hugh Henshall to route the Trent and Mersey Canal past his factory site. Wedgwood on this occasion called Henshall 'an inflexible vandal' as he insisted on taking the 'nearest and best way, or Mr Brindley would go mad'.[11] Tragically the Etruria works were demolished in 1968, but now an industrial heritage centre is growing up around Etruria Locks and the Etruscan Bone and Flint Mill. Housed in the mill buildings is a superb beam engine accredited to the firm of Bateman and Sherratt. The Sherratts were North Staffordshire millwrights and engineers who established a foundry at

The horsedrawn passenger trip boat *Birdswood* now operates public trips in the summer and charter trips all the year round.
Froghall Wharf Passenger Service

The canal between Froghall Tunnel and Wharf, c.1905.
J.R. Hollick/Manifold Collection

The view from Froghall bridge in 1905 which shows something of the cramped nature of the inner wharf area. The inlet (*to the right*) once led to an inner basin.
J.R. Hollick/Manifold Collection

The limekilns at Froghall Wharf where wagons could be loaded directly from the kilns. They were built after the 1847 tramway opened and most probably when the standard gauge line was extended from Froghall Junction. *The late Olive A. Dale*

The view from the same bridge in 1905 which shows something of the cramped nature of the inner wharf area. The inlet (*to the right*) once led to an inner basin.
J.R. Hollick/Manifold Collection

Etruria after their earlier enterprise with James Bateman in Salford. Perhaps one day, other North Staffordshire canal engineers like Hugh Henshall, Josiah Clowes, John Gilbert (Senior) and John Gilbert (Junior), will be afforded their rightful share of the honours. For too long the contribution of James Brindley to the development of the British canal system has been overrated.

The future of the Caldon Canal lies in the opportunities that it offers for recreational activities. Under the British Waterways Act of 1983, both the Caldon and Leek Canals were upgraded to 'cruising waterway status'; so ironically after all the years of neglect there is now a real need to guard against overuse and excessive commercialisation. Careful planning and controls should ensure that the canal does not become a 'liquid motorway'.

References

1. (Anon.), *Souvenir Brochure and Programme*, re-opening ceremony, (1974), p. 6.
2. Ibid., p.10 and *Leek Post and Times*, 21st February, 1963.
3. *Evening Sentinel*, 30th September, 1974.
4. Peter Lead, *Trent and Mersey Canal*, captions 80–82.
5. *Evening Sentinel*, 31st October, 1978 and 5th April, 1976.
6. Information supplied by Bill Young.
7. *Waterways News*, November 1979.
8. Information from the late Herbert Chester.
9. *Leek Post and Times*, 28th July, 1966.
10. *Waterways News*, November, 1988.
11. K.E. Farrer, op. cit., p. 197.

This fine picture of Froghall Wharf shows the railway/tramway interchange (*to the left*) and the canal loading area (*to the right*). *Author's Collection*

Chapter Seven

The Leek Canal and Rudyard Reservoir

When the canal company finally decided on the Churnet Valley route for their branch to Froghall in 1776, they effectively robbed the people of Leek of a direct link with the national canal network. This was one part of a double blow because there had been talk of an independent canal company building a canal to Leek. A survey had been made and subscriptions collected but the whole scheme came to nothing. So when, in 1793, the canal company showed an interest in using Rudyard Vale as the site for a reservoir, a number of the townsfolk of Leek determined that they could exploit the company's need and obtain a branch canal to the town. A letter written from Leek reiterates their past disappointment and predicts that the branch would bring:

> ... immense advantages ... to the Town and Neighbourhood — particularly in the article of coal, which in the Winter season the Inhabitants, especially the Poorer Folk, who cannot lay in stocks, are much distressed for.
> In these times of scarcity a very indifferent kind of coal is sold for 9d. a hundred, or 15s. a Ton. The Poor, who are only able to purchase about half a hundred at a time, from the backs of horses and asses, often pay after the rate of 2½d. for 25 lb. weight, or about 20s. a ton.
> By canal, we are assured, we shall have a sufficient supply of excellent coal, at a wharf near the town, at 8s. a Ton, or 5d. a hundred; and that the Poor will be allowed to purchase small quantities at these rates. The canal will also produce very important benefits to the Town and Neighbourhood, effecting a water communication with London, Liverpool, Bristol and Hull and the intermediate counties; and Leek will become the PORT, as it is the CAPITAL of the Moorlands.[1]

Hugh Henshall surveyed the route for a feeder channel down from the proposed reservoir site at Rudyard in December 1793 and presented his plan to the company in January of the following year.[2] As Rudyard Vale is to the north of the Endon Brook Valley and as the summit level of the Caldon Canal lay on the high ground south of it, an elevated crossing of the valley had to be constructed to preserve the respective levels. The feeder channel (over four miles in length) did not need to be very large in order to serve its purpose of bringing down water from the reservoir; but as a condition for allowing the channel to pass through their property, some of the landowners demanded that the canal company build a navigable branch to Leek. The landowners could afford to wait as indeed they had done for nearly 20 years, but the canal company was in a serious situation. They desperately needed additional supplies of water and they were also being troubled by the rival Commercial Canal scheme, which not only threatened its trade but could well have taken the water supply that the company was pursuing. The company's first Bill failed so they capitulated to the demands of the local landowners who won their branch coal. After this matter had been settled the Bill had a relatively smooth passage through the House of Commons.[3]

The work of making Rudyard Reservoir and the 2½ mile feeder channel to Leek was entrusted to John Rennie, who was also to be Consultant Engineer for the Leek Canal. He made his first visit to the area in February 1797, four months before the Act received the Royal Assent, a very clear indication of

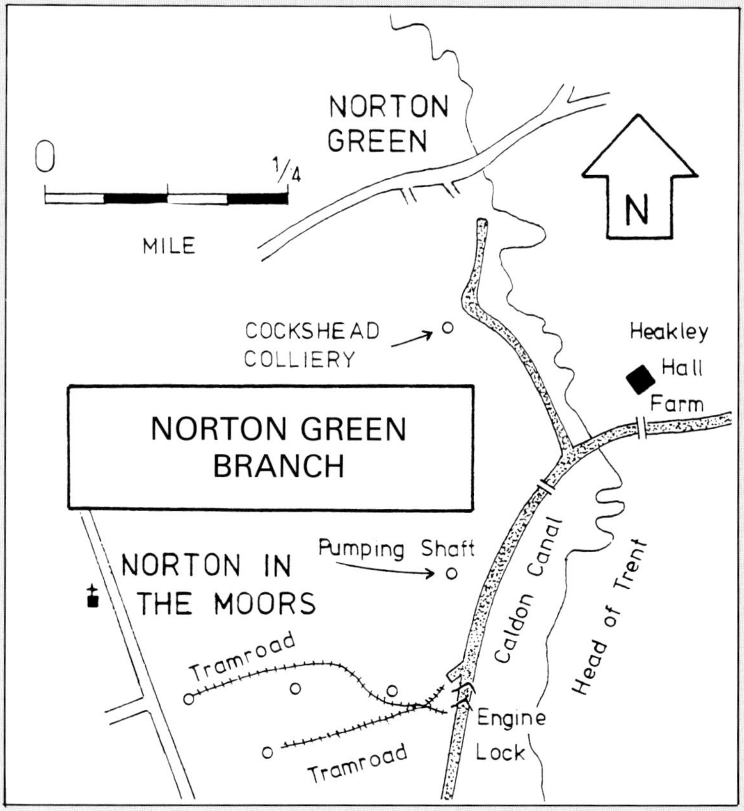
NORTON GREEN
0
1/4
MILE
N
COCKSHEAD
COLLIERY
Heakley
Hall
Farm
NORTON GREEN
BRANCH
Pumping Shaft
NORTON IN
THE MOORS
Caldon Canal
Head of Trent
Tramroad
Engine
Lock
Tramroad

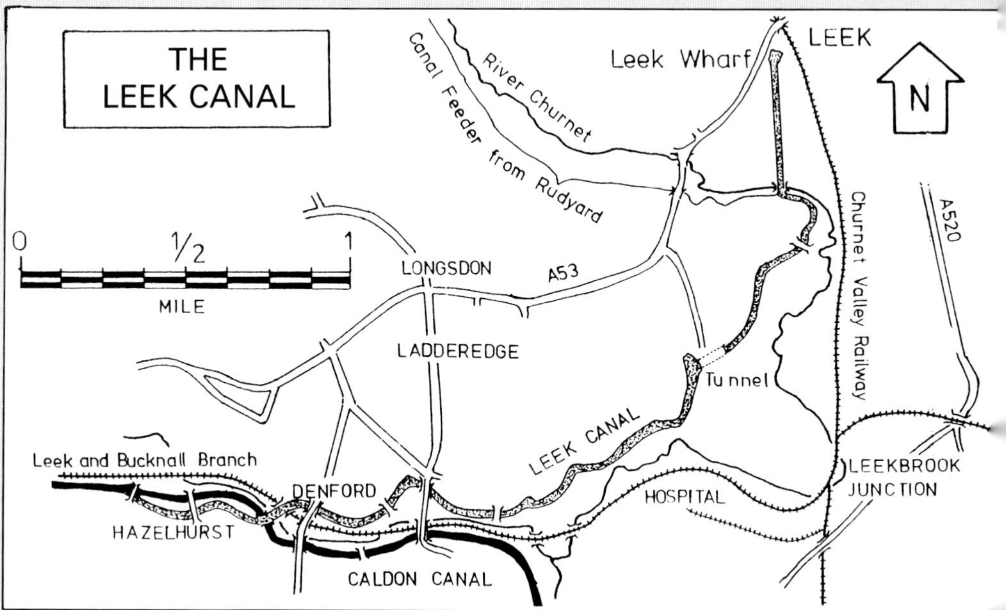
THE
LEEK CANAL
LEEK
Leek Wharf
River Churnet
Canal Feeder from Rudyard
N
Churnet Valley Railway
A520
0
1/2
1
MILE
LONGSDON
A53
LADDEREDGE
Tunnel
LEEK CANAL
Leek and Bucknall Branch
DENFORD
HOSPITAL
LEEKBROOK
JUNCTION
HAZELHURST
CALDON CANAL

the company's desire to see the project under way. Rennie largely endorsed Hugh Henshall's plan but had different ideas about the locks at Hazelhurst.[4] Work on the Rudyard site seems to have started in the summer of 1797 with James Potter as Resident Engineer, charged with the supervision of Thomas Peak and John Mansfield as the contractors.[5]

An earth dam, bow shaped and surfaced with stone on the water side began to take shape. John Farey reported that it was 'at the top 280 yds long, and at the bottom 220 yds, and is 36 ft high; its width (bottom) on the flat meadow is 100 ft, and at top 60 ft'. Large floods of water were to be dealt with by a 'stupendous weir of hewn masonry, 60 ft wide ... at the east end' of the dam; a precaution probably suggested by the floods of February 1795. Such floods seem to have been rare and between 1799 and 1807, the reservoir was only full once, another clear indication of the company's insatiable need for water.[6]

This demand was to continue to grow in direct relation to the increase in traffic on the canal and was only exacerbated by the need to provide for lockage on the Uttoxeter Canal. The reservoir created at Rudyard was nearly two miles in length; a quarter of a mile wide; and covered some seventy acres. It lay across the watershed of the River Dane and as John Farey observed 'the water might with ease be let out, to descend to either sea, with only [a] 13 ft cutting for a short distance at its northern end'. One of the feeder streams to the reservoir had formerly run into the River Dane, but had been diverted at Ryecroft Gate so that it flowed to the south. Later, under power granted in the Act of 1809, the company were allowed to build a further feeder across the watershed to bring the waters of the River Dane from a point below Danebridge into the older feeder at Ryecroft.[7]

The branch canal to Leek appears to have been undertaken after the reservoir was complete. John Rennie made a final tour of inspection in March 1801 and shortly afterwards the canal opened bringing with it the much needed water from Rudyard. Rennie had not wanted to build the three-rise lock staircase at Hazelhurst proposed by Henshall, preferring instead three separate locks. His advice was not accepted and the staircase was built at Hazelhurst, so that in years to come there were to be acute problems due to congestion and a wasteful use of water. Not until 40 years later were three new locks constructed here in the manner recommended by Rennie.[8] This involved diverting the Caldon to part of its original line, but as this was obstructed by the Leek Canal an aqueduct had to be built to allow it to pass under the Leek Canal, where the latter was already carried on an embankment over Endon Brook.

The canal company had always known that the traffic on the Leek Canal would never bring them any significant revenue and it is doubtful whether it ever reached the daily total of 10 boats, estimated by Rennie in 1797. Coal was always the most significant traffic and by 1834, the Woodhead Colliery Company had an Agent at Leek Wharf to co-ordinate sales of coal from their mine near Cheadle.[9] As the correspondent of 1793 predicted the initial demand for coal in Leek was purely domestic, but in 1826 the gasworks was erected to supply the town.

In the same year, Badnall's Silk Mill had gas lighting installed and three years later took delivery of the first steam engine to be used in the town's mills. By 1883 there were 36 steam driven mills employing some 4,000 people, although by this time coal could also reach the town by railway.[10] After the closure of the Uttoxeter Canal, the coal delivered to Leek came increasingly from the Norton area and this traffic continued until 1934. Henry de Salis made a curt summary of the economic significance of the Leek Canal around 1900, when he wrote: 'there is not much traffic on this branch'.[11]

The story might have been different if one particular scheme had been executed. In 1814 the Trent and Mersey Canal Company is said to have agreed to build a railway from the Leek Canal, up the valley to Bramcott (now Upper Hulme), passing between the Roaches and Ramshaw Rocks where an inclined plane was proposed to reach the collieries around Goldsitch Moss. From here, the line was to continue to Knotbury, before ascending to the collieries on Goyt's Moss and then descending to the quarries in Goyt's Clough (now more commonly called the Goyt Valley). The Goyt Quarries were leased by Thomas Pickford to Richard Wilson, a London stone merchant, who dealt in paving and building stones. Wilson proposed that if the Trent and Mersey Canal Company built the railway and with other canal companies ('southward to London') agreed only to charge toll at ¼d. per ton per mile, he would guarantee income in tonnage at 7 per cent of the cost of the railway. He made similar proposals to the proprietors of the Cromford, Chesterfield and Peak Forest Canals in May 1814, and in a limited way he seems to have foreseen the Cromford and High Peak Railway of 1825.[12] Nothing came of Wilson's proposals, but John Farey mentions that stone quarries were being worked at Bramcott, possibly by Thomas Pickford who already had the quarries at Consall Forge.[13] It seems very likely that this scheme may have been linked with the railway enterprise that became the North Stafford Railway of 1815, (see *Chapter Ten*). Further research may well reveal a link as Pickford's involvement in local quarrying and the associated trade becomes better understood.

The last commercial traffic on the Leek Canal was a trade in tar from Milton and this survived until 1939. Five years later, Charles Hadfield records, the London, Midland and Scottish Railway Company obtained parliamentary powers to abandon the canal. The short section of the canal to the north of the Churnet Aqueduct was purchased by Leek Urban District Council in 1957 and they promptly filled it in.[14] The rest of the branch, in common with the Caldon Canal, was just left to decay until both were rescued by the restoration package. Since then a serious set of problems were discovered in the Leek Canal tunnel. Large voids were discovered throughout the tunnel behind the stonework lining, coupled with a flattening of the tunnel arch at the south portal and a general deterioration of the stonework at water level. The response by British Waterways Board was both swift and positive; and they began remedial work in July 1984. The deformed section of the arch was exposed by removing part of the hillside. The defective stonework (at water level) was replaced with concrete blocks and the voids were infilled with cement. Extreme care had to be exercised as both of the portals were listed as being of architectural and historical interest, so only repointing and general cleaning work were possible. The whole programme was completed in December 1984 at a total cost of £200,000 and Sir Leslie Young reopened the tunnel in the following April.[15]

References

1. *Derby Mercury*, 14th November, 1793. Copy supplied by Alan Jeffery.
2. SRO: D593/V/3/29.
3. Hadfield, op. cit., p. 200.
4. Rennie's Notebook, Box 26, loc. cit.
5. John Farey, op. cit., p. 442; and 37 Geo.III cap. 81, Royal Assent 6th June, 1797.
6. Ibid., pp. 442–443. (The reservoir was completed in 1799.)
7. 49 Geo.III cap. 73, Royal Assent 20th May, 1809; and John Farey, op. cit., p. 442.
8. Date on the Denford aqueduct.
9. William White, *History, Gazetteer and Directory of Staffordshire*, (1834), p. 708.
10. Harold Bode, *The Leek Canal and Rudyard Reservoir*, (1984), p. 6.
11. Henry de Salis, *Bradshaw's Canals and Navigable Rivers of England and Wales*, (1904), p. 276.
12. John Farey, op. cit., p. 448.
13. SRO: D593/K/1/5/4.
14. Harold Bode, op. cit., p. 6.
15. Information supplied by British Waterways Board.

The former warehouse buildings at Leek Basin as they were in 1958.
The late Peter Norton

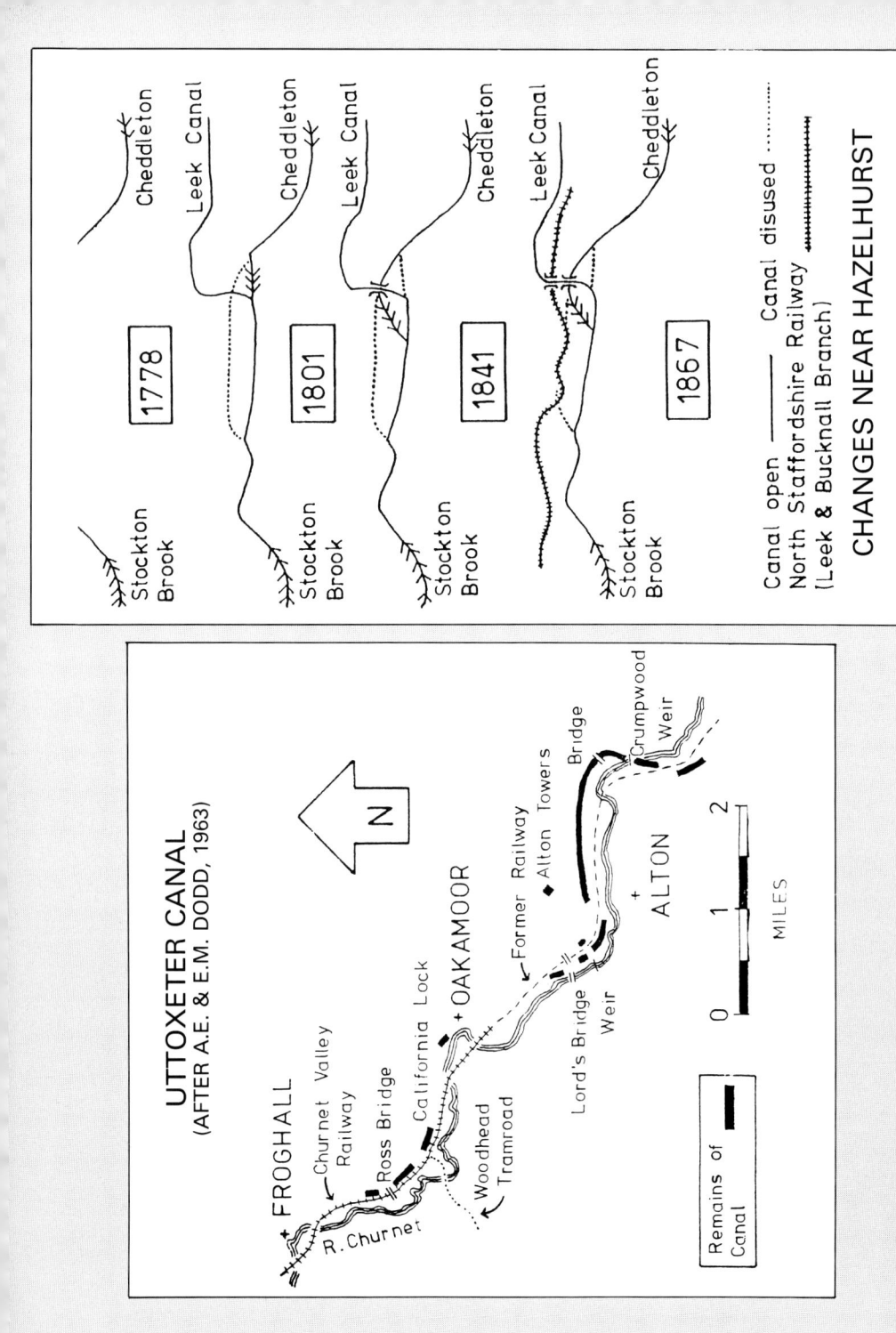

UTTOXETER CANAL
(AFTER A.E. & E.M. DODD, 1963)

CHANGES NEAR HAZELHURST

1778 / 1801 / 1841 / 1867

Canal open ——— Canal disused ·········
North Staffordshire Railway ++++++++
(Leek & Bucknall Branch)

Chapter Eight
The Uttoxeter Canal

The Trent and Mersey Canal Company were in many ways forced to build a branch canal to Uttoxeter by the proposals for the rival Commercial Canal. The germ of this project can be traced back to the proposals for the so called Dilhorne Canal, projected from Monks Bridge on the River Trent to the Dilhorne Collieries (near Cheadle), via Tutbury, Marchington and Cheadle.[1] In comparison the Commercial Canal was to be far more ambitious and seen as a real threat by the Trent and Mersey Canal Company. The promoters of this scheme seem to have been Sir Nigel Bowyer Gresley (a canal and colliery owner), the Burton Navigation, representatives of the Ashby and Chester Canals and certain pottery manufacturers anxious to promote a competitive route. The proposal was for a barge canal from the Chester Canal at Nantwich (a broad canal providing a connection to the Dee at Chester and the Mersey via the Wirral line) through a tunnel to join Sir Nigel Bowyer Gresley's Canal in Apedale; then across the Trent and Mersey Canal near Burslem and the Caldon Canal near Bucknall; and by the Cheadle Coalfield to Uttoxeter; and then down the Dove Valley to join the broad section of the Trent and Mersey Canal below Horninglow. A further section would have taken it across the River Trent below Burton so as to form a junction with the Ashby Canal.[2]

This rival scheme offered the Potteries an alternative route to both east and west, avoiding the Duke of Bridgewater's Canal altogether. The use of barges would have brought economies in relation to bulk carriage that would have crippled the Trent and Mersey Company. The Duke of Bridgewater recognised a common enemy in the scheme and pledged his support for the Trent and Mersey's Uttoxeter Canal plan.

However, the canal company's main agent, William Robinson did not pursue his intention to secure the aid of Thomas Gilbert, explaining that: 'I should have waited on Mr Gilbert on Monday in hopes of prevailing on him to sign some letters to his friends which would no doubt be very useful but the account Mr Yeoman's gave me of his declining state induced me to think such application improper'.[3] As was common in such disputes the atmosphere became heated and the tactics almost machiavellian. An anonymous hand-bill was circulated entitled *Observations upon the Committee of Subscribers to the proposed Commercial Canal Scheme*; and later John Gilbert, Junior, signed a declaration with 42 other pottery owners disassociating themselves from a declaration supposed to have been made by a meeting of pottery manufacturers in support of the Commercial Canal. Thomas Gilbert was sufficiently recovered to sign an answer to the Commercial Canal scheme in June 1796 and he attended a proprietors meeting in October of the same year.[4]

A crucial meeting was held at Uttoxeter in August 1796 with Josiah Wedgwood II in the chair. This meeting was a direct response to an earlier meeting held in the town by the promoters of the Commercial Canal scheme. Their meeting was reported as follows:

> ... many respectable Land-owners had attended that Meeting by special Invitation, and which by advertisement was expressly declared to the public and convened for the purpose of considering the design in question and the expediency of applying to Parliament. Yet when the Land-owners began to inquire what advantages were likely to accrue from the project by way of compensation for the waste and injury it would occasion, they were hastily told that no interrogatories would be answered, and none but friends of the measure were to speak at the Meeting. By means of which unprecedented conduct every degree of investigation was prevented, and the resolutions then ready prepared were put and carried without examination or discussion ... THE Land and Mill-owners now assembled having taken the whole of the case into consideration, and having duly deliberated upon the same,
>
> DO resolve – THAT the scheme in agitation, as far as they are at present able to judge, will be highly injurious to much valuable property, consisting of inclosed Farms and of Mills adapted to the uses of Manufacture, without affording a prospect of any adequate advantages either public or private, and therefore ought to be opposed and they do agree to oppose the same accordingly.

If this indeed is a fair and accurate summary of the earlier meeting, then it is clear that the promoters of the Commercial Canal scheme had realised that time was not on their side. The Trent and Mersey Company had marshalled their supporters well and they were prepared to make promises to ensure the support of key landowners. They gave way to the landowners in the Leek area and courted those further to the south with the promise at the same meeting that the Uttoxeter Canal would: 'facilitate the conveyance of Lime, Coals and other articles, [and] will be of great utility to the Land-owners and Neighbourhood in general'.[5] The company also promised that they would widen the canal from Fradley to Harecastle, which caused the Grand Junction Canal to drop its support for the 'Great Commercial Canal'. When the rival scheme was 'dead and buried' all thoughts of a widening programme were conveniently forgotten.[6]

The meeting at Uttoxeter thanked Wedgwood for 'his impartial conduct and attention to the business of the day'; and resolved that 'a branch of Canal from the CALDON CANAL at Froghall to or near Uttoxeter, and another branch to Hanging Bridge near Ashborn' be built by the Trent and Mersey Company. The battle was not quite over and the rival promoters had not yet given up. They deposited their plan at Stafford on 29th September, 1796, exactly one day before the Trent and Mersey Company presented the plan for the Uttoxeter Canal to the same clerk.[7] There now only remained the matter of parliamentary powers and the canal company by then had the odds stacked in their favour.

This final hurdle was overcome in March 1797 but already John Rennie had visited the area to check and approve the plans.[8] The Uttoxeter Canal was to be built virtually along the line laid down in the deposited plan, although Rennie had recommended some minor changes. Nevertheless there were no real problems with either landowners or engineering difficulties, just a reluctance by the company to build a canal which never promised to

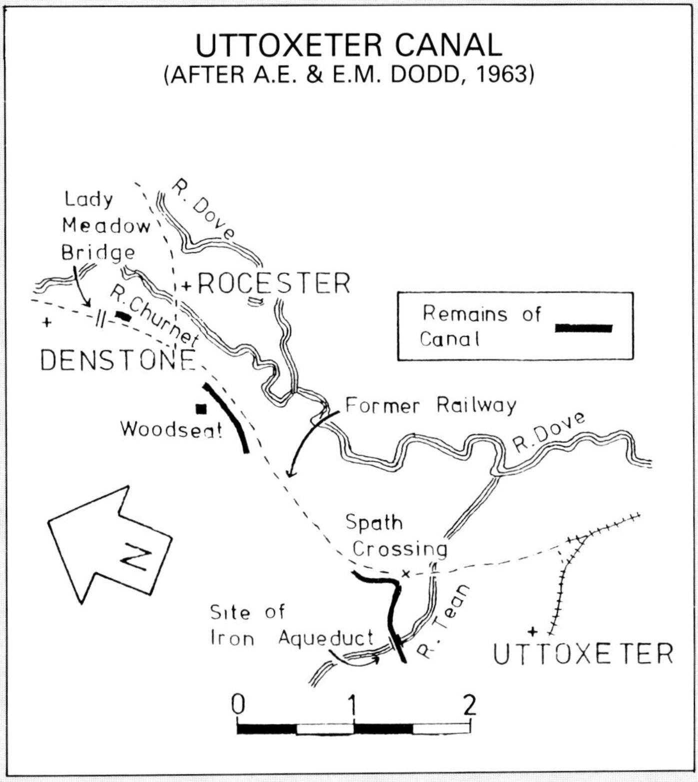
UTTOXETER CANAL
(AFTER A.E. & E.M. DODD, 1963)
Lady
Meadow
Bridge
R. Dove
ROCESTER
R. Churnet
DENSTONE
Remains of
Canal
Woodseat
Former Railway
R. Dove
N
Spath
Crossing
Site of
Iron Aqueduct
R. Tean
UTTOXETER
0
1
2

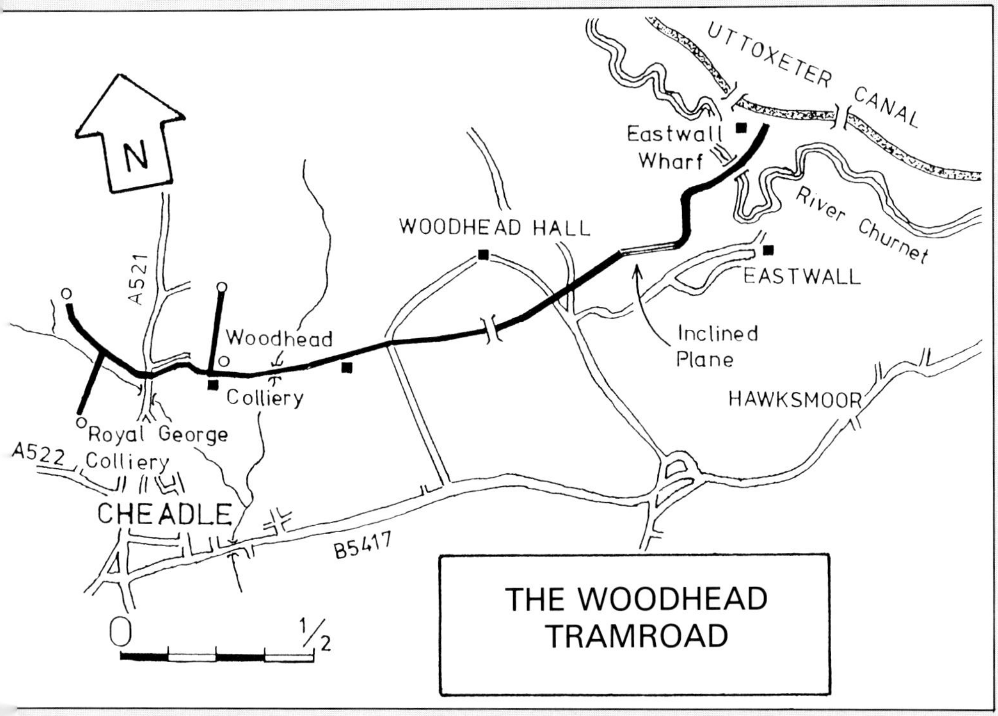
UTTOXETER
CANAL
N
Eastwall
Wharf
River
Churnet
WOODHEAD HALL
EASTWALL
A521
Woodhead
Inclined
Plane
Colliery
HAWKSMOOR
Royal George
Colliery
A522
CHEADLE
B5417
THE WOODHEAD
TRAMROAD
0
1/2

be a commercial success. During the summer of 1800 the company were seriously considering building a railway instead of the proposed canal. They advertised in the *Staffordshire Advertiser* (31st May, 1800) for:

> Persons inclined to contract for the forming and stoning the ground for a Railway from Froghall to the Turnpike Road at Stub-Wood (Rocester), and from the said Road to Spath near Uttoxeter, in two distinct Lots, according to a plan and Specification now laying at the canal office, Stone, may send their Proposals to the Committee at the said office, on or before the 20th June next.

A horse-drawn railway would have cost a quarter of the expense of the canal and not drawn away any of the precious water supply that the company jealously guarded. The notion of building it in two 'distinct Lots' is also significant; as Stubwood is the point where the turnpike roads from Uttoxeter and Ashbourne converge, so that the company could have drawn traffic from both towns at half the cost of the complete railway. By this time the company had also given up the proposed branch canal from Rocester to Hanging Bridge (Mayfield), a mere 1½ miles from Ashbourne.

The company seemed perfectly happy to let matters rest at this although John Rennie was brought back to make further recommendations in April 1801. This may have resulted in a report that suggested some minor changes in the projected line near Alton and these were incorporated in a clause of a further Act passed in 1802 (42 Geo.III cap 25, Royal Assent 15th April, 1802). There also seems to have been a 'dispute' between the Earl of Shrewsbury and the Cheadle Brass Company on the one hand, and the canal company on the other. Charles Bill had reported in 1797 that 'the Earl of Shrewsbury has no objections to the intended canal, if his tenants have not'.[9] But after tenders were invited for the building of the canal in July 1802, the attitude of the Cheadle Brass Company (with works at Alton) changed. They kept a close eye on the construction work 'to examine whether the Navigation Compy make use of, or divert any stream or streams of water belonging to the River Churnett'.[10]

Meanwhile, the Earl's attitude seems to have changed somewhat. Faced with a proposal that the canal company 'take the mill pond of the wire company at Alton, and replace it with a parallel one', he declared that it would 'disfigure the valley'.[11] This whole matter seems to have been conducted along very gentlemanly lines and again it is easy to detect the relaxed attitude of the canal company with regard to the infant branch. The discussions went on for two years and culminated in an agreement signed by all three parties in April 1809.[12] Another and almost certainly the major factor was that of cost, as revealed in the Act of 1809 (49 Geo.III cap. 73, Royal Assent 20th May, 1809):

> Whereas the said Company have made and completed all the works authorized by the said recited Acts, except the Canal from Froghall to Uttoxeter, which they are proceeding in with the utmost Expedition; but to enable them to finish it a further Sum is necessary to be raised . . . not exceeding Thirty Thousand Pounds.

It is almost as if this agreement closely followed by the clause in the Act removed the last excuse that the company could cite. Progress had been pitifully slow, especially when it is considered that it was five years before the company advertised for tenders. According to John Farey, the section between Froghall and Oakamoor was built between 1807 and August 1808; work starting five years after tenders had been invited. This first part was three miles long and the next two miles to Alton were completed by May 1809.[13] The remaining 8½ miles to Uttoxeter were completed in just over two years and by great good fortune a very complete account of the opening ceremony has survived:

> On Tuesday, [3rd September, 1811], the Uttoxeter Canal was opened with every demonstration of joy which the inhabitants of that town and neighbourhood could devise. Early in the morning the bells announced the approaching jubilee, and continued at intervals throughout the day to ring peals of gladness. Soon after breakfast the lads and lasses from neighbouring villages in their holiday dress began to assemble in the Market Place, where they were joined by the principal inhabitants, and the whole then marched to the canal basin, preceded by a most excellent band of music playing favourite airs.
>
> Here a most enchanting view presented itself; a spacious wharf furnished with every requisite building and accommodation for the convenience of trade, manufacture, and agriculture; together with an ample supply of coal and lime to answer the demands of the town and adjacent country. In the adjacent basin lay two elegant pleasure boats for the use of the proprietors and their friends, and soon after eleven o'clock embarked these with four or five other boats fitted up for the occasion, displaying taste, particularly that which conveyed the band. The necessary arrangements being made, the *Prince Regent* boat took the lead, and proceeded in good style to the beautiful cast-iron aqueduct over the River Tean, where the company disembarked for a short time, and then continued on their course.
>
> After passing Rocester, where upwards of 300 persons belonging to Mr Briddon's cotton works attended in holiday dress to add to their testimony of joy, the boats arrived about two o'clock at the grand weir across the River Churnet, at Crump Wood, a distance of about six miles from Uttoxeter, amid the acclamations of immense crowds of spectators, who occupied every bridge, and lined the sides of the canal, whilst others kept pace with the boats. On an eminence, commanding delightful and romantic views of woods, rocks and water, were placed suitable accommodations for the entertainment of the company. About 150 persons partook of a cold collation, provided in a superior style by Messrs Chamberlain and Garle of Uttoxeter.
>
> The cloth being drawn, several appropriate toasts and sentiments were given by the Chairman, H. Webb, Esq., and drank with the utmost good humour and harmony. Among the songs was one written for the occasion by Mr Goodall, and sung with great effect by Mr Clarke and others.
>
> About five o'clock the company embarked on their return to Uttoxeter, attended by the band and numerous assemblage of spectators, rending the air with shouts of joy. The weather was remarkably fine, which greatly contributed to render the surrounding country uncommonly Sublime.[14]

The townsfolk of Uttoxeter had every reason to celebrate as they had waited 10 years for the canal company to start work on the canal, and a further four years for the construction work to be completed. The canal company could also draw some satisfaction for they had pulled off one of the greatest stonewalling exercises in canal history. By 1818 an extensive network of coal agents and delivery points had developed along the canal.

The Woodhead Colliery and Tramroad of 1841.

Courtesy The Staffordshire Record Office and E. Heaton and Sons

The Woodhead Colliery Company, Sparrow and Hales (Cockshead Colliery) and Thomas Kinnersely (Kidsgrove Collieries) were all established at Uttoxeter Wharf.[15] But despite this provision: 'coal was (still) brought to the town regularly over the backs of mules and donkeys, ... on what might be called pack saddles, and this caused a considerable business in breeding mules in the neighbourhood of Alton and Cheadle'.[16] The Woodhead Colliery also supplied wharves at Alton and Combridge; and by 1834 the Hazlecross and Ford Green Coal Companies were also supplying the wharf at Uttoxeter. There also appears to have been quite a healthy seasonal trade in lime with the principal kilns at Oakamoor and Uttoxeter, all of which were being operated by John Leigh in the 1830s.[17]

Francis Redfern relates how: 'a dock-yard for the construction and repair of boats was opened, and a works in the same vicinity was commenced for the manufacture of ... crude wood vinegar'.[18] Cheshire cheese and Welsh slate were also on sale at the wharf with a major outgoing trade in locally produced tiles, bricks and pipes.[19] The fact that a windmill is mentioned by the canal in 1811 is probably not coincidental, for as another writer noted, the town had: 'a very considerable corn-market; the grain is not pitched but sold by sample, and large quantities of corn are sent to different parts of England by canal'. He also made a general comment on the impact of the canal on Uttoxeter:

> The wharf belonging to the Grand Trunk Canal Company with several large warehouses enclosed by a brick wall, and situated at the northern extremity of High Street, has contributed much to the prosperity of this small but flourishing town, which is thickly inhabited, and exhibits undoubted proofs of the opulence of its merchants, tradesmen, and inhabitants in general.[20]

Despite such glowing assessments much of the traffic on the Uttoxeter Canal was linked to agriculture, so that in the slump that followed the Napoleonic Wars trade went into decline. The idea of a branch canal from Rocester to Ashbourne was revived in 1813, and again in 1824 when it was proposed that it should be continued through Ashbourne to Little Eaton on the Derby Canal. These projects, and the 1839 proposal of a canal south from Uttoxeter to the Trent and Mersey Canal at Burton, came to nothing.[21] Of them all, the last was probably the most practical as it would have created an avenue for the export of Caldon limestone into the East Midlands, as well as providing an alternative route to the Potteries.

The surviving evidence suggests that the Woodhead Company and the Cheadle Brass Company (with works at Alton and Oakamoor) made most use of the canal. The Woodhead Colliery was connected to a wharf at Eastwall (on the canal) by a tramroad constructed between 1808–09.[22] The cost of this work seems to have stretched John Leigh and John Clark beyond their resources; so that in 1812 they offered for sale: 'one half of the ... Rail Road, leading between the Woodhead Colliery and Uttoxeter Canal, with waggons and business annexed thereto'.[23]

It is not known whether anyone took up this offer, but the partners weathered these financial and associated legal problems. John Leigh's finances were sufficiently recovered by 1815 for him to become involved in

RATES OF TONNAGE

ON THE

Caldon, Leek, & Uttoxeter Canals,

AT ONE PENNY PER TON PER MILE.

Commencing 19th November, 1832.

A table of Tolls on the Trent & Mersey's Caldon, Leek and Uttoxeter branches.

Courtesy Charles Hadfield

the North Stafford Railway Company (see *Chapter Ten*). The Woodhead tramroad may have become disused at the time of Leigh's bankruptcy in 1841, but it was certainly abandoned when the Uttoxeter Canal was closed in 1847 or 1848. Woodhead Colliery was taken over by Leigh's agent, William Bowers who increasingly sold his coal from a railway wharf on the Cheadle Froghall Road (A521). The section (including the incline near Eastwall) that descended into the Churnet Valley was described as 'having been disused for years' in 1877, when a proposal was made to repair the tramroad and use 'Locomotives and other steam engines'. The author of this idea was Willaim Shepherd Allen, who wished to convey coal along the tramroad to sidings to be built in the valley alongside the Churnet Valley Railway.[24]

In 1844 the Churnet Valley Railway was proposed with a route that paralleled that of the canal and in places it was proposed that the railway should be built in the canal bed itself. The North Staffordshire Railway Company wanted to take over the canal company, but this had to be investigated by the Select Committee on Railway and Canal Amalgamations. The committee sat in 1846; and in evidence the canal company declared that they were already thinking about closing the Uttoxeter Canal, as it was costing them 'something like £1,000 beyond the return, each year to keep it up'.[25] So it would appear that even without the railway, the canal was already doomed after a life of only 35 years. Subsequently, to facilitate the building of the railway, portions of the canal were infilled, which in years to come caused flooding on the line. A famous photograph taken in 1958 (and to be found in Robert Keys' book *The Churnet Valley Railway*) shows a 2–6–4 tank locomotive entering Alton Towers Station with water half way up its wheels; it looks just as if the canal has put in a return appearance.

Long stretches of the canal can still be traced today by the determined walker, who will discover the remains of locks and bridges, as well as the impressive Crumpwood Weir. The incessantly meandering River Churnet complicated the construction work and this weir was part of a novel solution to the problem of effecting a crossing. Boats could cross in the comparatively still water behind the weir, while the horses crossed by means of a bridge further upstream. This technique later became common in the United States but in this instance the inspiration may have been found locally, as, before 1778, the River Churnet (near Consall Forge) had been used in a similar way to continue the line of the Caldon Canal. The other notable engineering feature was the cast-iron aqueduct which carried the canal over the River Tean, just to the north of Uttoxeter. The abutments still survived but the aqueduct itself has gone. The late W.G. Torrance recollected seeing the disused route of the canal and the fate of the aqueduct:

> In my own boyhood, not only the large Canal warehouse (then the Stay Factory) but the name 'Dockyard Farm', the empty basin where barges once floated, the whole length of the Canal holding water on which we skated after severe frost, but filled with many water-plants during summer, all these still remained in 1900 to show what the Canal had been. Finally, I recall the loud explosions which occurred when dynamite (my first knowledge of this) was used to break up the 'beautiful aqueduct' over Tean Brook into manageable portions to be sold for Old iron.[26]

References

1. John Farey, op. cit., pp. 360–361.
2. *Abraham Rees's Manufacturing Industry (1819–20)*; Edited by N. Cossons, (1972), Vol. I, p. 356.
3. SRO: D554/162.
4. HRL: s.p.138.6 and *Staffordshire Mercury*, 25th June and 8th October, 1796.
5. Hand-bill from the Heathcote Papers, lent by David Dyble.
6. Jean Lindsay, *The Trent and Mersey Canal*, p. 82.
7. SRO: Q/RUm/17–Q/RUm/19; and the Heathcote Papers.
8. Rennie's notebooks, loc. cit.; and 37 Geo.III cap. 36, Royal Assent 24th March, 1797.
9. SRO: D554/90.
10. A.E. and E.M. Dodd, 'The Froghall–Uttoxeter Canal', *North Staffs. Journal of Field Studies*, Vol. 3 (1963), p. 61.
11. SRO: D554/90.
12. A.E. and E.M. Dodd, op. cit., p. 61.
13. John Farey, op. cit., pp. 445–446.
14. *London Chronicle*, 19th September, 1811; reprinted in *Uttoxeter Advertiser*, 5th May, 1926.
15. W. Parson and T. Bradshaw, *Staffordshire General and Commercial Directory*, (1818), pp. 263–267.
16. Francis Redfern, *History and Antiquities of Uttoxeter*, (1886), p. 389.
17. William White, op. cit., pp. 727, 758, 762 and 767.
18. Francis Redfern, op. cit., p. 389.
19. W. Parson and T. Bradshaw, op. cit., pp. 260–265 and John Farey, op. cit., p. 454.
20. *Staffordshire Advertiser*, 20th July, 1811 and W. Parson and T. Bradshaw, op. cit., p. ci.
21. *Derby Mercury*, 16th September, 1813, 8th September, 1824 and 19th June, 1839.
22. SRO: D239/M/2435.
23. *Staffordshire Advertiser*, 20th June, 1812.
24. SRO: D239/M/2600.
25. Bertram Baxter and A.P. Voce, Railway and Canal Historical Society Tour Notes, No. 13, (1963); *Consall Plateway, Woodhead Tramway and Uttoxeter Canal*, p. 4.
26. W.G. Torrance, *Following Francis Redfern*, part VIII, p. 17.

A length of the former Uttoxeter Canal at Lord's Bridge (Alton) in 1958.
The late Peter Norton

Chapter Nine

The Caldon Low Railways

In total four 'railways' were built between Froghall Wharf and the Caldon Low Quarries, and in turn each carried limestone down to the Caldon Canal between 1778 and 1920. They were all 'railways' but there were differences in the types of rails employed, engineering practice and modes of operation, such that the terms 'tramroad (or plateway)' and 'tramway' are more appropriate for the last two lines. Similarly, the dating and labelling of each 'railway' sometimes raises problems. Dr J.R. Hollick was the first transport historian to describe the routes of the various railways and to place them in a chronological context. In his article in the June 1937 *Railway Magazine*, he described the '1777 original line and the 1780 reconstruction'; the '1802 plateway' and the '1849 Cable Railway'. At the time that Dr Hollick was writing documentary sources were very limited and it is only in recent years that it has become possible to prescribe accurate dates for the 'opening' of each railway.

Reference to the dates when these railways became operational is the only satisfactory way of making mention of them without causing further confusion. The first three railways were built using parliamentary powers granted in 1776, 1783 and 1802 respectively; but the last railway was constructed simply by the consent of the relevant landowners. The engineers responsible for the last two lines are known, but there is still doubt as to whom the credit for the first and second railways should be accorded. Bearing all this in mind, the following arrangement has been adopted in this book (based on the date when each line became operational): the first railway is called the '1778 line'; the second/reconstruction: '1785 line'; the third railway (John Rennie's tramroad): '1804 line'; and the fourth railway (James Trubshaw's tramway): '1847 line'. I believe that such an arrangement clarifies the development of this fascinating mineral railway system.

When claiming railway 'firsts' great care must always be taken to qualify what is actually being asserted. It has long been known that the Middleton Colliery Railway was the first railway to be built using powers granted by an Act of Parliament in 1758. Yet it was not generally realised that the Caldon Low railway of 1778 was the first railway using iron rails to be constructed with an authority derived from a legislative enactment, albeit essentially a canal Act. Since the appearance of the first edition of this present work the significance of this railway has been placed in a national context by Leslie James. In his *A Chronology of the Construction of Britain's Railways, 1778–1855*, he begins his detailed listings with the 'Froghall Tramway' (Caldon Low Railway) of 1778.

There would have been no need to build any of the Caldon Low railways if the earlier plans for a route paralleling the Leek–Ashbourne road had been adopted. The problem identified in 1775–1776 was how best to connect the terminal of the canal at Froghall Wharf (430 ft above sea level) with the Caldon Low quarries (some 1100 ft above sea level). Obviously, the options were limited and locks were clearly impossible. The best and somewhat novel solution was the construction of a railway and here again it is not difficult to see the influence of John and Thomas Gilbert. Both brothers were

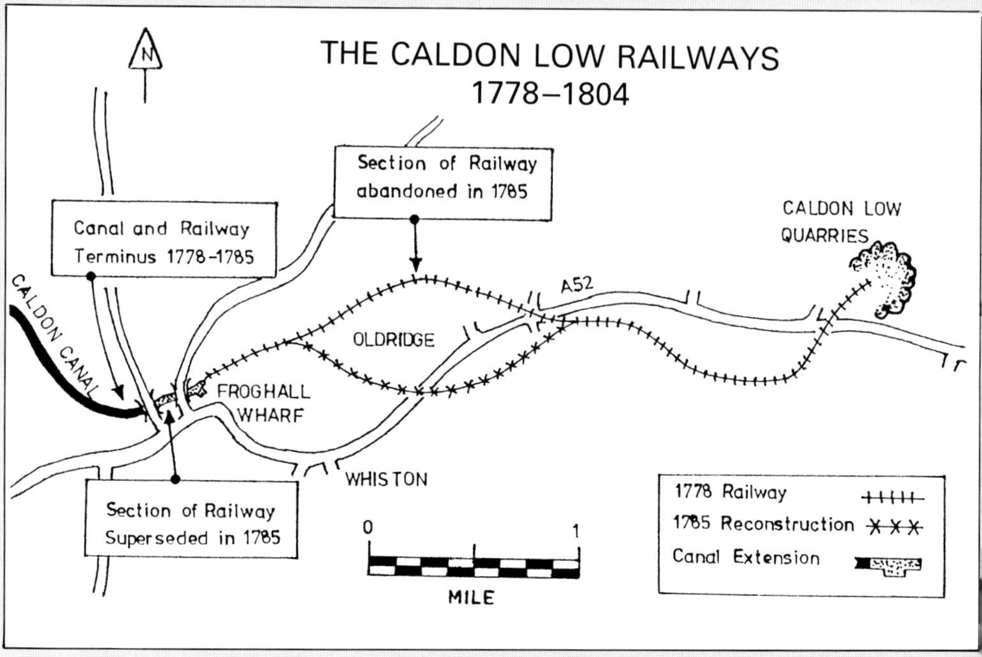
THE CALDON LOW RAILWAYS
1778–1804
N
Section of Railway
abandoned in 1785
Canal and Railway
Terminus 1778-1785
CALDON LOW
QUARRIES
CALDON CANAL
A52
OLDRIDGE
FROGHALL
WHARF
WHISTON
Section of Railway
Superseded in 1785
0
1
MILE
1778 Railway
1785 Reconstruction
Canal Extension

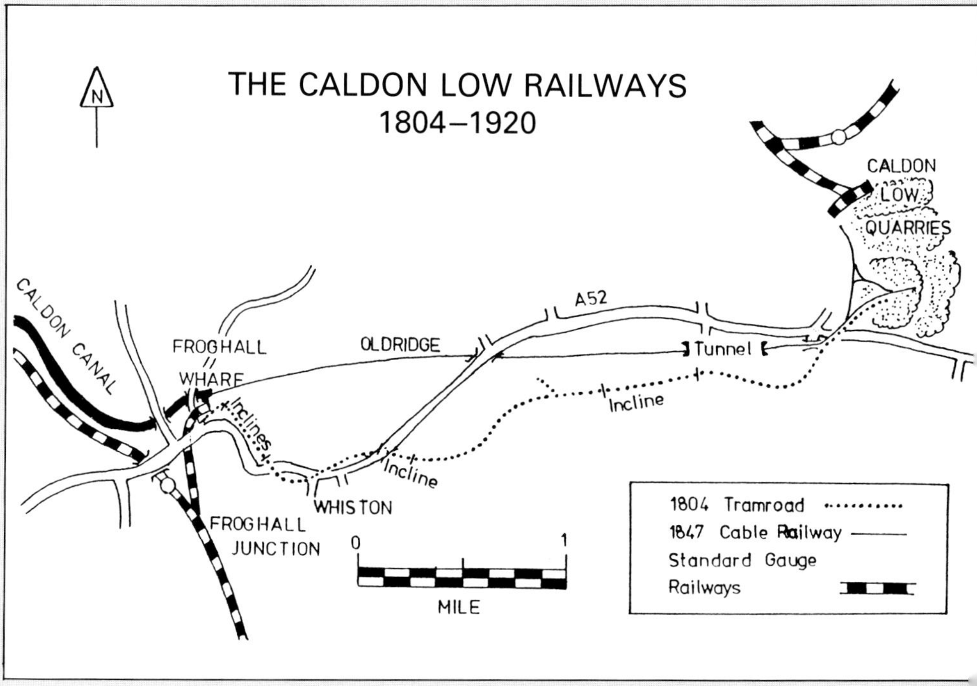
THE CALDON LOW RAILWAYS
1804–1920
N
CALDON
LOW
QUARRIES
CALDON CANAL
A52
FROGHALL
WHARF
OLDRIDGE
Tunnel
Inclines
Incline
Incline
WHISTON
FROGHALL
JUNCTION
0
1
MILE
1804 Tramroad
1847 Cable Railway
Standard Gauge
Railways

partners in the Donnington Wood collieries in Shropshire, which lay on the Coalbrookdale railway system. They knew that they worked in that setting and probably believed that the terrain between Froghall and the quarries was comparable. As the leading expert on early railways has remarked: 'The Caldon line seems to belong more to the Shropshire tradition. The track is pure Shropshire'.[1]

John Gilbert may also have been responsible for laying out the line of the railway for he was a gifted engineer and had been brought up in this area. Hugh Henshall had no previous experience of railway construction, but as he gave evidence to Parliament on both the canal and railway, then he must have been involved in the preparation of the final plan for the line. When in 1778 the Chesterfield Canal Company built a railway from Norbriggs Colliery to their canal, Hugh Henshall was the Engineer, so possibly he was making use of experience gained on the first Caldon Low railway.[2] Whoever the author of the route was, it turned out to be an unfortunate plan. The railway opened in December 1778 and within a year Edward Ball (of the Navigation Office, Stone) was writing that: 'the Railway has been repaired but in Frost the Waggons slide so much that is is almost impossible to carry anything upon it'.[3] John Farey expressed the problem more precisely when he wrote that the railway: 'appears to have been set out, before the true principles of this branch of Engineery [sic] was well understood and was very crooked, steep and uneven in its degree of declivity in different parts'.[4]

The most expedient solution to this problem was partially to rebuild the railway. The worst section across Shirley Hollow was abandoned and replaced with a more workable line employing easier gradients. This new section ran on the opposite side of the Shirley Brook, passing through Harston Wood and then up across Whiston Common. Parliamentary powers for this 'second railway' were included in the Act of 1783 (23 Geo.III cap. 33, Royal Assent 17th April, 1783); this also allowed the canal to be extended for a further 540 yds to the present Froghall Wharf, so that a comparable length of the first railway became obsolete in that part of the valley.

The bulk of the work was undertaken in the accounting period from June 1784 to June 1785 when £2414 9s. 3d. was spent on improving the railway, so that in March 1785 it was reported that the company was 'completing a new Railway from the canal at Froghall'. They lost no time in selling off part of the 'old railroad' to Ralph Oakden, who took possession on 4th August, 1785.[5] Although the records are not complete, it is possible to calculate that it cost the company an average of nearly £600 a year to maintain the railway during the period 1785–1791; and this figure does not take into account sums like the £834 3s. 11d. spent on further improvements in 1790.[6] Doubtless the reconstructed line was better, although not much and it is hardly surprising that the company were soon to start giving serious thought to a third and more efficient railway.

Both the 1778 and 1785 lines were laid with flat iron rails fixed on top of wooden rails after the Shropshire tradition. They were described as being,

> ... three feet long and had two holes, at 18 inches apart, to receive the wooden pins which fastened them down, or rather confined them in their places on the

Part of the track of the first Caldon Low Railway in Shirley Wood as it was seen in 1952. *J.R. Hollick*

The path of the first railway, 1778 emerging from Harston Wood as captured on film in 1952. *J.R. Hollick*

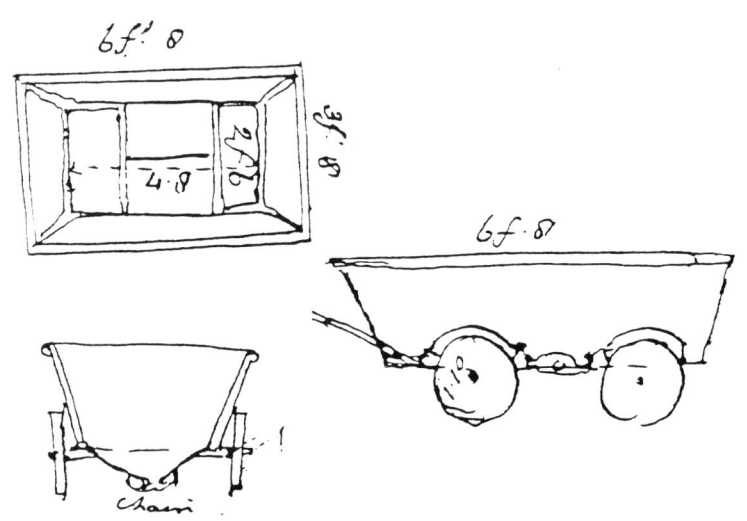

John Rennie's drawings of the wagons used on the Caldon Low railways between 1778 and 1804.

A view of the trackbed of the 1804 tramroad at Cotton, in 1936.   *J.R. Hollick*

This is a 1936 view of Caldon Low Railways where at the Upper Cotton Plane, the 1804 tramroad crosses the original 1778 railway.   *J.R. Hollick*

wooden rails; at one end there was a triangular projection, and at the other a similar notch which fitted into each other ... and opposite the holes, the rail which was about 1¾ inches thick and weighed about 42 lb., was made wider to strengthen that part; yet, with all this precaution, such rails were very liable to break in two at the pin holes, as well as to loose their connecting triangular pieces.[7]

The first of the railways was said to have cost £1 per yard, suggesting a total cost of around £6,000 for the whole line. The only motive power was provided by horses, which, writes John Farey, 'each week (made) 3 journies on 4 of the days, and 2 journies on the other 2 days, drawing down each time 66 cwt of Limestone'. All wagons were the property of the quarry owners, but this was a principle that was not established until late in 1779.[8] Indeed there seems to have been no recognised operating system on the first two railways before 1787, when Thomas Gilbert agreed to organise the traffic 'down the railway'. The result was a management committee resolution:

> To form sundry Regulations respecting the passage of waggons and other carriages on the Railway, between the termination of this branch at Froghall, and the Limestone Quarries at Caldon Low, which they apprehend will be proper to be passed into BYE LAWS.[9]

It seems remarkable that it took nearly ten years to regulate the use of the railways, meanwhile it is easy to imagine how improper use added to the reasonable wear and tear on the lines. Apart from having to buy their own waggons, the quarry owners also had to pay for and build the branch railways that actually went up to the quarry faces. Having said this there were exceptions and in 1786 the company built a branch railway for Henry Copestake at a cost of just under £95.[10]

When John Rennie was in the area to advise on the Leek and Uttoxeter Canals, he also examined the second Caldon Low railway on 5th February, 1797. He made a series of notes that in the main described the waggons then in use, but he was obviously struck by the steep gradients on the line and the method of working waggons down from Caldon Low. Apparently, waggons were brought down on a gravity run with the waggoner sometimes sitting on the brake.[11] Three years later Thomas Yates made a detailed survey of the proposed route for a tramroad from Froghall to Caldon Low and John Rennie visited the Froghall area in April 1801 to examine the ground in relation to the plan. He made nine recommendations all of which show a keen eye for the shape of the terrain, although in two instances it involved longer inclined planes than originally proposed. At Froghall Wharf he proposed that 'the waggons should be emptied and tipped by Ballance frames — so as to tip when the waggon is loaded and return when empty'.[12]

Work on the third railway (or to be more technically correct — tramroad) started in 1802 and was completed in 1804, during which period large quantities of 40 lb. (gang rails) and 49 lb. (road rails) were purchased from the Butterley Company.[13] John Farey provides a very complete and fascinating account of Rennie's tramroad which he examined in 1808, opening with the reasons for its construction:

> The inconvenience of these steep and imperfect Railways occasioned the application in 1802 for the Act for a new line of railway, to be laid double, on stone

The track bed of the 1804 tramroad near Hoftens Cross photographed in 1936.
J.R. Hollick

Hoftens Cross in 1936, with the 1847 line running over the bridge and the 1804 and 1778 lines on the track to the right.
J.R. Hollick

blocks with a moderate and proper slope, and with intervening Inclined-planes; and in the following year the same were carried into effect under Mr Rennie and are among the most complete works of their kind in Britain. On the wharf at Froghall, a stock of Limestone is kept, ready for loading the Boats; which is shot thereon from 10 tippling-machines; and the draw-holes of 4 large Lime-kilns are also near at hand, for loading Boats with burnt Lime. Short Rail-ways from the Tipples above mentioned, lead to the bottom of the lower Froghall Plane, which is 65 yards long, with a perpendicular rise of (29) feet: the Trams loaded with Limestone are let singly down one of the Rail-ways hereon, and the empty Trams, or loaded with Coals, are drawn up the other, by chains that wind contrary ways round a large horizontal Drum, furnished with a regulating Brake, at the top of this Plane.

From the top of the lower Plane, there are branch Rail-ways laid to Tipples, for emptying Limestone and Coals at the tops of the Lime-kilns, mentioned above, that are situated on each side of this Plane: and from these and the top of the lower Plane, a Rail-way of about 50 yards long, with a rise of 8 inches per Chain (4/11ths of an inch in a yard), conducts to the bottom of the upper or great Froghall Plane, which is 303 yards long, with a rise of 240 feet.

Under a large open Shed at the top of this Plane, there are fixed two strong wooden pulley wheels turning on vertical axes, and round these, and round other pulley wheels at the bottom of the Plane, a strong endless Chain (weighing 72 cwt.) passes, and over cast-iron guide pulleys, so as to conduct the Chains over the two Rail-ways on the Plane, on the middle parts of which, it drags, on smooth Cast-iron saddle-shaped blocks, fixed between the Rails, for the purpose; to the descending side of the chain 5 loaded Trams of Limestone are hooked, by short lengths of chain, and to the ascending side as many Trams, in part loaded with Coals, or empty, are hooked; and their too rapid motions are prevented, by a brake, acting on one of the pulley wheels.

At the top of this (Froghall) Plane, a person resides to take care of it, and has at his door a Weighing-machine, on which each Tram of Limestone is weighed, before it is attached to the great chain, and launched on to the Plane, by removing a stop that prevents its descending by accident: from the accounts that I saw here, it appeared, that the weight of Limestone in each Tram vary from 22 to 30 cwt. average 25 cwt. (of 120 lb.).

From the top of this (Froghall) Plane, a Rail-way proceeds ¾ mile (passing Lees Colliery) with a rise of 4/11ths inch per yard, to the foot of the Whiston Plane, which is just NE of the Copper Works: this Rail-way, at 60 or 70 yards from the last (Froghall) Plane, began to be cut some yards deep in the 1st Grit Rock, with a SE dip into the Whiston Coal-trough.

The Whiston Place is 150 yards long, and rises 75 feet, having similar pulley Wheels, a Chain and brake, to those above described: from its top a Rail-way again proceeds about 1 mile, with a rise as before, to the bottom of the Upper Cotton Plane, which is 294 yards long, and rises 130 feet, and whose endless chain passes around a single large pulley Wheel, whose axis is so inclined, as to suit the inclination of the Chain, and has a brake, etc. as before. In order to obtain an uniform slope for this Plane (a thing no ways essential), a deep-cutting, 30 feet deep, has been made at its lower end, and its upper end is banked up, to the height of 15 feet.

From the top of this upper Plane, the Rail-way is again continued, with the same degree of rise as before, 1¼ mile, into Caldon Low Lime Quarries. Near the top of this Plane, the Rail-way again crosses the 1st Grit Rock with a WSW dip, and under the Turnpike Road is a deep cut in Limestone Shales; at Haughton Cross there is a Sale Coal-yard, with 4 turning-plates and Tipples, for shooting Coals into Carts, for

The bearded gentleman in this photograph is John Billings who worked on the 1847 tramway for a staggering sixty-seven years. *Tom and Will Billings*

A train of wagons on the 1847 tramway near Harston Rock in 1905. The trains consisted of a maximum of nine wagons, each of which carried 6 tons of limestone. *C.M. Beardmore*

the use of the Inhabitants and the private Lime-kilns of this elevated district.

The Trams used on this Rail-way and Plane, have stout lower side-pieces of wood, which project at each end, and are hooped with iron, which just meet together, and receive the shock when the trams overtake each other (i.e. collide), at the bottoms of the Planes, and on other occasions of their striking each other: one Horse draws 12 of these Trams loaded, down these Rail-ways, and as many empty ones up, but extra Horses are necessary, I believe, in bringing up Coals. The hours of working at these Planes daily, are from ½ past 5 o'clock in the morning to the same hour in the afternoon, in which time 18 dozen of Trams of Limestone are usually let down, perhaps containing 270 Tons of Limestone.[14]

Despite his obvious admiration for Rennie's railway, Farey could not resist making his own recommendations for an alternative or supplementary railway scheme. He proposed a railway from a point near the Alton aqueduct (on the Uttoxeter Canal), firstly eastwards then directly northwards up the valley towards Wootton Park. Skirting to the east of Ramshorn it would have given access to proposed limestone quarries in the Weaver Hills 'without so many Inclined-planes and such great expenses as attends the Caldon-Low Railway'. He even thought that the cost of inclined planes might be avoided 'by tunnelling some distance at the head of the valley (to) reach the Limestone, to begin a quarry, as was done at Crich'.[15]

The third railway, according to William Robinson: 'very much increased the trade in limestone', although it is very difficult to establish exact figures for the period. For a 48 week season in 1795, the quarry owners bound themselves to deliver 40,000 tons of limestone, which gives a weekly traffic on the railway of around 830 tons.[16] This figure was bettered when the third railway came into use after 1804 and by 1834 a weekly average of one thousand tons of limestone passed down the railway, although when working to capacity the system could deal with 250–270 tons each day, William White records.

One clear advantage to the canal company of Rennie's line was that it cost less to maintain than the earlier two railways. Maintenance costs stood at about £600 a year around 1790, which may be compared with a repair bill of just over £374 in 1829. In the same year the relatively paltry sum of £157 was spent on the maintenance of all three of the company's 'Pottery Railways'; and from this it is possible to judge the heavy use being made of Rennie's Caldon Low Railway.[17]

By 1834 the canal company were leasing and working the quarries on their own account and paying: 'two fifths of the rent to the Early of Shrewsbury, one fifth to the Reverend Thomas Gilbert, and the remaining one fifth to Mrs Wilmott, J. Bill, Esq., and Mr George Woolliscroft.[18] Seven years later the canal company were seeking a more favourable arrangement regarding their working of the quarries. They were being pressed by competitors in the lime trade and they needed to increase output, or more accurately to find a way of moving more limestone — as much as 1000 tons per day. One serious problem with Rennie's railway was that it was laid with short flanged rails made of cast-iron, so they were liable to break under heavy loads or simply as a result of continual usage. Once any rail broke, the whole system was halted until that rail could be replaced; and with a system that was more

This family snap, taken after the last tramway closed in 1920, shows that for most of its route the line was only laid with three rails.
B.H. Snow

It was only necessary to have four rails at points where trains of wagons would pass each other; the empty wagons being drawn up by the weight of the full ones on the descent. *J.R. Hollick/Manifold Collection*

The incline in 1933 at Caldon Low Quarry.
H.C. Casserley

than thirty years old and heavily used such breakages became increasingly more common.[19]

In 1836 the canal company decided that a completely new line should be built incorporating the most recent advances in railway engineering. It was to be built along a completely new route so that Rennie's tramroad could continue in use until simply superseded by the new tramway. James Trubshaw (the company's Engineer) was given the job of negotiating with landowners along the proposed route and in 1842 he presented his plan to the company's management committee. The fourth railway was to be an impressive project. James Trubshaw had previously worked as a contractor with the Grand Junction Railway and built the 14 mile stretch of the railway between Stafford and Whitmore Heath. He used this experience on the Caldon project, so that his tramway exhibited the scale and confidence of a modern railway line. The total cost was estimated at £14,289 10s. 2d. which included: retaining walls, footbridges, culverts, a major embankment through Harston Wood, a tunnel 330 yds long, ten bridges, road diversions, drains, gates, laying the track and iron rail sleepers. Work began in 1842 and Trubshaw himself laid the first brick in the tunnel on 17th April, 1844.[20]

Trubshaw was concerned to get the new railway completed as soon as possible as Rennie's line was thought to be on its 'last legs'. Yet when you examine the bridges on this line, it is clear that Trubshaw did not cut any corners and in these it is possible to see the expression of his skills as a builder and architect. The work on this line was started by the orders of the canal company but it was to be completed for the North Staffordshire Railway Company who bought out the canal company with effect from 15th January, 1847. By July of that year the 'new' railway was complete and the following advertisement in the *Staffordshire Advertiser* heralded the stepping up of production:

NORTH STAFFORDSHIRE RAILWAY
COMPANY
TRENT AND MERSEY NAVIGATION BRANCH

To Limestone Getters, Quarrymen, and other contractors

The Directors of the North Staffordshire Railway are desirous of Letting the Getting of their Limestone in their Quarries at Caldon Low, and the conveyance of the same to the Canal Wharfs at Froghall, by means of the new line of railway provided for that purpose.

The contracts will also have to keep in repair the said railway and all works and implements connected therewith.

H.B. Farnell
Manager
Trent and Mersey Canal Office
Stone

The fourth railway to traverse the route between Froghall and Caldon Low was a railway in the full sense of the term, using flanged wheeled wagons but still at a gauge of 3 ft 6 in. It was single track although there were three rails, the central one being common to both the descending and ascending

The entrance to Trubshaw's Tunnel seen here in 1936. This took the Caldon Low Railway 1847 line.
J.R. Hollick

This is an official North Staffordshire Railway Company postcard of 1905, showing the tramway system within the Caldon Low Quarries. The special tank wagons brought up water from Garston, for the quarry engines.
J.R. Hollick/Manifold Collection

lines. Passing loops (where the central rail split into two rails) allowed the trains to pass each other. It was worked by cable and gravity in four sections. The sections were: Froghall Wharf; Froghall Wharf to Oldridge; Oldridge to Tunnel End; and Tunnel End to Caldon Quarries. Although the railway was worked by cables on the inclines, within the quarry workings horses were used to marshall the waggons. Most of this work was taken over in 1877 by two 0-4-0 saddle tank locomotives christened *Frog* and *Toad*. They were joined by a third locomotive in 1901. This locomotive was called *Bobs* after Field-Marshall, Lord Roberts V.C., who had reinforced his own reputation and salvaged some national prestige from the Boer War.

The fortunes of the Caldon Low quarries reached a zenith during the life of this last railway. Sometime after 1857, a standard gauge line half-a-mile long was laid in the bed of the former Uttoxeter Canal from Froghall Wharf to Froghall Junction on the Churnet Valley Railway. The canal and this branch railway dealt with the 1,000 tons of limestone conveyed daily down the tramway, in trains of between five and nine waggons each carrying 6 tons of limestone. Each train was controlled by several brakemen who were responsible for engaging or unhooking the cables on the inclines. At Froghall Wharf the limestone was crushed, burnt or loaded into narrow boats and trains. The line remained in regular use until 25th March, 1920 when it was officially closed, although one informed source has asserted that odd waggons of limestone were sent down to keep the limekilns at Froghall supplied until the contract with the operator lapsed.[21]

Seldom when examining the history of canal or railway systems does the opportunity arise to study the careers of the individuals who maintained them. Associated with the Caldon Low tramway was John Billings who followed in his father's footsteps and became a platelayer. John began work for the North Staffordshire Railway Company in 1853 at the tender age of 12, his first job being to help dismantle the derelict 1804 tramroad. He worked with his father on the last railway receiving wages of 2s. 8d. a day in 1869 and he continued to work as a platelayer until his retirement in February 1920 at the age of 79. In recognition of his 67 years of service, the Traffic Committee of the railway company granted him a 'Retiring gratuity under very special circumstances' of £25. A month after he retired the last tramway was closed and in May of the same year he died at Wharf House, Froghall.[22]

Even before the closure of the cable railway in 1920, Caldon Low had been so extensively quarried that the workings were moving farther away from the original western workings towards Waterhouses. On 1st July, 1905, a ¾ mile-long standard gauge branch was opened from the new Leekbrook–Waterhouses branch (built to connect with the narrow gauge Manifold Valley Light Railway) at Caldon Junction, to give better access to the new quarry workings.[23] At one time, it was proposed to extend this branch down the course of the tramway to join the Churnet Valley line at Froghall, but the cost of conversion and working promised to be prohibitive. From this time onwards an increasing amount of limestone passed down the new standard gauge line, avoiding the need to tranship to the railway or boats at Froghall Wharf. As far as the tramway was concerned it was living on borrowed time and it may have closed even earlier but for World War I.

A side view of the third locomotive purchased in 1901 and christened *Bobs* after Field Marshall Lord Roberts. *The late Olive A. Dale*

A party of officials at the Caldon Low Quarries in 1902 for the Coronation Blast. *Toad* had brought up the two special passenger wagons from the top of the tramway incline. *J.R. Hollick/Manifold Collection*

After 1918 the quarries were generally less active and with the railway amalgamations of 1923, they became the property of the London Midland and Scottish Railway Company, which abandoned sections of the workings. According to this company's records, the quarries ceased to be profitable after 1925 and they came to consider them a burden rather than an asset. In 1934 Messrs Hadfield of Sheffield, a subsidiary of the Derbyshire Stone Company took a lease of the quarries. On 12th March of the same year, the Manifold Valley Light Railway closed, although the spur from Caldon Junction remained open to serve the goods yard at Waterhouses until 1943. After this, the standard gauge line from Leekbrook to Caldon Low became essentially a mineral line serving the quarries. The three small locomotives at the quarry had outlived their usefulness by May 1936, when they were taken from their shed (still in North Staffordshire Railway Company livery) and scrapped.[24]

Today, the quarries are worked by Tarmac Road Holdings for road metal and by Associated Portland Cement who have a large works at Caldon. Early in 1970, the Caldon Low sidings (capable of taking 100 wagons) were handling 6,250 tons of stone in 4 daily trains for either ballast or roadstone. Loads of 1,000 tons are a common sight on this line, although because of severe gradients anything in excess of 500 tons is taken to Leekbrook on a second working and the two sections then coupled for the run to Stoke. How much longer this line will survive is uncertain as road transport has proved to be more competitive.

References

1 M.J.T. Lewis. *Early Wooden Railways*, (1970), p. 285.
2 Ibid., p. 281 and Jean Lindsay, op. cit., p. 55.
3 WSL: HM 37/19.
4 John Farey, op. cit., p. 436.
5 WSL: HM 37/19 and SRO: D554/84.
6 WSL: HM 37/19.
7 *Abraham Rees's Manufacturing Industry (1819–20)*; edited by N. Cossons, Vol. I, p. 326.
8 John Farey, op. cit., p. 436 and SRO: D554/84.
9 WSL: HM 37/19.
10 WSL: HM 37/19–20.
11 John Rennie's Notebook, No. 26.
12. Ibid., and SRO: Q/Rum/27.
13 Derbyshire Record Office: Butterley Company Records, Furnace Ledger B, fo. 111. (Information from Philip Riden.)
14 John Farey, op. cit., pp. 436–439.
15 Ibid., pp. 447–448.
16 SRO: D554/90 and SRO: D554/84.
17 WSL: HM 37/19.
18 William White, op. cit., p. 729.
19 Information from Will Billings.
20 Anne Bayliss, op. cit., p. 73.
21 J.R. Hollick, op. cit., pp. 437 and 440.
22 Information from Tom and Will Billings; and from Dr J.R. Hollick.
23 Rex Christiansen and R.W. Miller, *The North Staffordshire Railway*, (1971), pp. 118–123.
24 This information comes from a paper 'The Caldon Low Tramways', read to the Cheadle Historical Society in 1954 by Dr J.R. Hollick.

The horse in this photograph serves as a reminder that all the marshalling of wagons was carried out by horses until 1877. In that year, the company bought two 0-4-0 saddle tank locomotives soon christened *Toad* and *Frog*.

Author's Collection

Caldon Low sheds in 1936, on the old 1847 line showing side-tipping wagons and water tank wagons.

J.R. Hollick

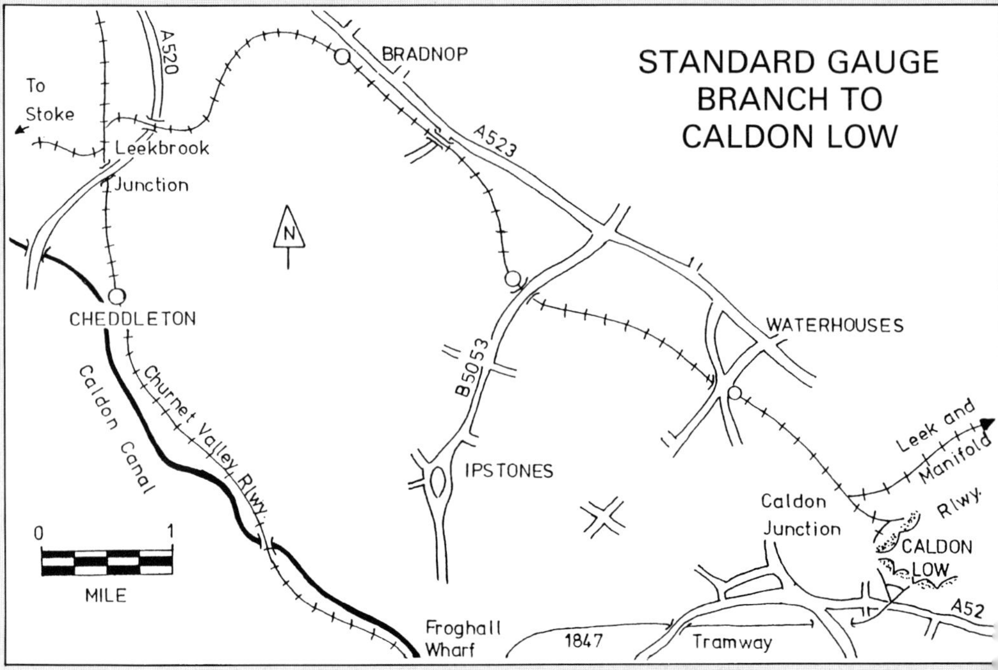
STANDARD GAUGE BRANCH TO CALDON LOW
BRADNOP
A520
A523
To Stoke
Leekbrook Junction
N
CHEDDLETON
Caldon Canal
Churnet Valley Rlwy.
WATERHOUSES
B5053
IPSTONES
Leek and Manifold Rlwy.
Caldon Junction
CALDON LOW
0
1
MILE
A52
Froghall Wharf
1847
Tramway

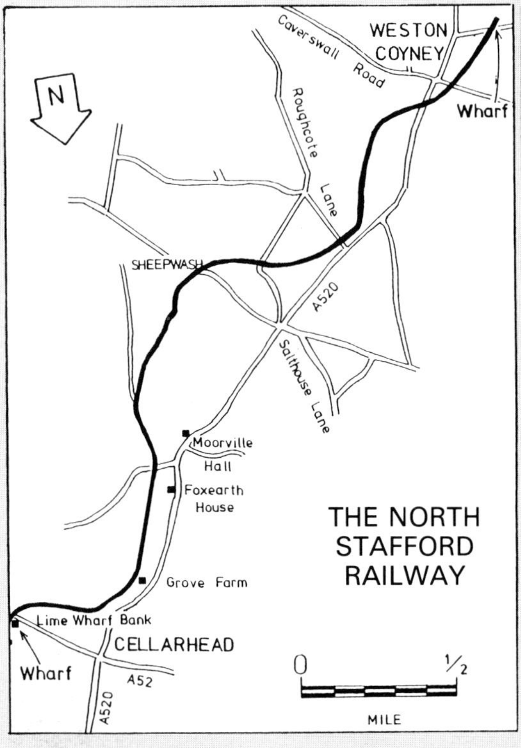
WESTON COYNEY
Caverswall Road
Wharf
N
Roughcote Lane
SHEEPWASH
A520
Salthouse Lane
Moorville Hall
Foxearth House
THE NORTH STAFFORD RAILWAY
Grove Farm
Lime Wharf Bank
CELLARHEAD
Wharf
A52
A520
0
1/2
MILE

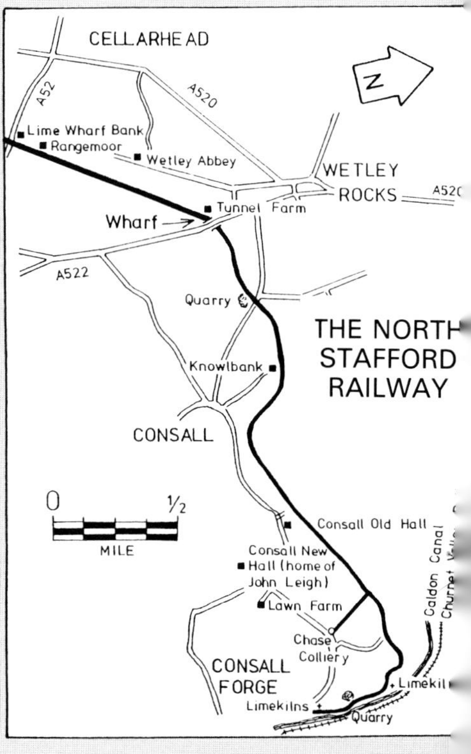
CELLARHEAD
N
A52
A520
Lime Wharf Bank
Rangemoor
Wetley Abbey
WETLEY ROCKS
A520
Tunnel Farm
Wharf
A522
Quarry
THE NORTH STAFFORD RAILWAY
Knowlbank
CONSALL
0
1/2
MILE
Consall Old Hall
Consall New Hall (home of John Leigh)
Lawn Farm
Chase Colliery
CONSALL FORGE
Limekilns
Quarry
Caldon Canal

Chapter Ten
The North Stafford Railway of 1815

There is an unquestionable fascination in searching out and exploring the routes of old tramroads. Beckoned by diverse relict features and place names, the late J.D. Johnstone set out to explore and describe one such early railway. The particular line ran from Consall Forge to Weston Coyney and little can be added to his description of the route, despite more recent and extensive fieldwork. Johnstone referred to the line as the 'Consall Plateway', but he was working without any significant documentary evidence and only scanty oral traditions to supplement his fieldwork. He was never to know that he had explored and described the route of the 'North Stafford Railway', built between 1815 and 1819.[1]

Most tramroads were either built by canal or colliery companies; but this one is the more noteworthy as it was built by an independent railway company akin to the Surrey Iron Railway Company of 1801, although the similarities should not be over-emphasized. The Surrey Iron Railway Company built its tramroad under powers embodied in an Act of Parliament, whereas the North Stafford Railway Company built its railway by the consent of landowners and subject to wayleave agreements. One of these documents has survived in a draft form. Dated 2nd January, 1815, it was drawn up between George Granville, Marquis of Stafford, and his son, Earl Gower, of one part, and the partners in the North Stafford Railway Company of the other part, of whom only George Lambert Clifford is named. The tramroad was to run from the Caldon Canal in Consall Wood to Mill Field Lane (Weston Coyney), which matches the remains traced by Johnstone and later fieldworkers.[2] 'The Iron Railway or framed waggon way' ran in the main over land which belonged to the company's proprietors, except for a key area to the west of Longton. The relevant parcels of land belonged to the Marquis of Stafford, head of the richest noble house in Britain whose principal seat was at Trentham Hall.

The draft agreement (or lease) is couched in a fairly positive style, but matters were far from being settled. On 7th March, 1815, James Loch (Chief Agent to the Marquis) wrote to Mr Burgess (Colliery Bailiff for the Meir Heath and Longton Mines), requesting more information about the railway scheme; and in particular asking if he knew of any plan to extend it to the canal company's railway in Longton, other than 'through Lord Stafford's Millfield gate farm'. The very same day, Loch wrote to Thomas Fenton, one of his Lordship's legal advisers; and his letter provides a very complete insight into the rationale behind the railway scheme:

> I went to Lane End (Longton) today to endeavour to learn the truth of the story respecting the projected railway, and the following was the amount of my information. Thomas Pickfords have taken some stone quarries in the neighbourhood of Ipstones, in consequence of the Leek canal being often dry in summer and soon frozen in winter their carriage of the stone to London is extremely precarious, they have therefor projected this railway and all the landowners are in favour of the adoption of the measure — the estate said to be sold to them by Sir John Heathcote is bought in the name of one Clifford and Sir John it is added is doing everything to get the railway to go through his land. I am further told that the Grand Trunk (Trent

and Mersey) have the power, by an Act in being of extending their Lane End Railway through Lord Stafford's Mill Fieldgate farm near Stirrup's house.

If all or any of the above statement be correct you will see that we have no power (even if it was advisable) to prevent their getting their railway forward. It were better therefore, to get them to go through Lord Stafford's land than let them go through any other persons, but from what I can learn there is no coal which can be brought along this railway which can enter into competition with his Lordship's coal as they are unsuited for the Potworks and his Lordship's for economical purposes. May I beg you to endeavour to ascertain how far any of the above particulars are correct and what upon the whole would be my best mode of proceeding. If there should be any truth in it perhaps I had better see the Pickfords at once. Will you be good enough to learn from (Thomas) Sparrow whether the Grand Trunk have the power I have above alluded to.

Later that same month, Loch instructed Burgess not to say that Lord Stafford 'will certainly support the Railway through Mill Fieldgate', until he had obtained full details of the scheme. Further facts were provided by George Lambert Clifford, whose place of residence was given as 'Consall'. Clifford disclosed that the partners only wished to cross three of his Lordship's fields, which prompted a detailed survey of the proposed route by two of Lord Stafford's agents. They were to also make enquiries about 'the new coalwork' and the possible effect of the railway on his 'Lordship's Lime' trade. This almost certainly refers to Chase Colliery (near Consall Forge) and the limekilns (a little to the north of Consall Forge) in Consall Wood. This same letter also reveals that 'Mr Bishton decidely refused the (earlier) application' regarding the proposed railway.[3] As George Bishton had been replaced by Loch as Chief Agent to the Marquis in 1812, this reference proves that the railway scheme was at least three years old by 1815.[4]

On 13th April, 1815, Loch responded to a second letter from Clifford and in this he relates how he had consulted Lord Stafford on the matter, who felt it would be advantageous to himself as well as being 'beneficial to the County'. In a rider, Loch adds that 'others in the neighbourhood of Lane End (were) afraid their interests and Lord Stafford's would be hurt by this measure', so he would make further enquiries. He then proposed to meet Clifford with a view to reporting back to his Lordship, but in the meantime despatched Suther (Agent for the Trentham and Newcastle estates) to discuss the progress of the scheme. After Suther's visit, Loch wrote again saying his Lordship was ready to meet 'your wishes immediately', but 'excepting coal from amongst the articles to be carried along the railway' as it could 'materially injure those coals with which Lane End is now supplied'. He also suggested 'the use of all the railway for himself (Lord Stafford) and his estate', instead of any form of monetary compensation for land taken or for wayleave. The exclusion of coal was not acceptable to George Clifford and his partners, who pressed the matter and on 2nd May his Lordship waived this condition. Loch as the ever cautious and loyal agent noted the possible dangers of this relaxation when he wrote: 'I trust you are very certain you are not letting in any northern horde upon us'. He continued to press the partners to allow Lord Stafford free use of the railway, but took care to stress that this would only be used to move items for building repairs and for the general improvement of the estate. A further proposal also appears at this juncture with Loch seeking the option to construct 'side branches from it (the railway), one to Normacot and the other towards Trentham'.

On the same day, but in another letter, Loch makes reference to the 'North Stafford Railway' — the first time that this name is used. He is still seeking concessions for Lord Stafford, but there is a definite shift in emphasis and the railway partners appeared to be gaining the upper hand. One of Loch's proposals betrays a more reconciliatory approach: 'if (his Lordship) brings Limestone along the railway to burn at Lane End for the purpose of Sale that in this case he must pay toll like others — if to burn for his own use not'. Mr Suther was instructed to 'learn the sentiments' of the canal company about the proposed railway 'as it may materially effect the trade of their Caldon branch'. Loch's example of the lime traffic and the fears about lost canal tolls reveal that this railway was to be a major avenue for local trade.[5] As the major source of limestone was intended to be the quarries at Mixon Hay, then the use of Caldon Low limestone would have fallen off with a corresponding drop in tolls paid on the Caldon branch.[6] Towards the end of May 1815, Loch wrote to Messrs Caldwell, Sparrow and Robinson as representatives of the canal company 'about extending their Railway from Longton'. He warmly recommended that they form a junction with the North Stafford Railway 'as the Trade in stone and in Lime would be very considerable indeed', but took care to point out that the proposed railway was a means of supplying lime and stone to the area between Consall and Longton. He clearly recognised the conflict of interest between the two parties and the threat to the receipts of the canal company.[7]

On 1st June, John Leigh described by Suther as 'one of Mr Clifford's partners' is mentioned for the first time, although he was probably the prime mover in the scheme having purchased the Consall estate in 1811.[8] The North Stafford Railway Company were still not convinced that Loch was supporting their aim of 'getting the Navigation Railroad up to its point at Millfield Lane (Weston Coyney)'. Such fears were unfounded as both the Marquis of Stafford and Loch were doing all they could in the face of the opposition centred around William Robinson, the canal company's chief agent. Loch wrote to him directly and pointed out that even if the Caldon Canal,

> ... should be effected in the way you seem to fear, I should entertain no doubt of the increased exportation of stone mentioned in my last letter to you adding to the general trade of the canal and I am informed that the Caldon branch of the Canal is often frozen when the main Trunk remains navigable. These are however matters for the consideration of the company only the advantage which Lord Stafford's estates will derive from the arrangement is incalculable especially from the increased facility of which Lime will be obtained.

The opposition of the Trent and Mersey Canal Company stifled the original plan by the simple device of refusing to co-operate. It was clearly not in their best interest to facilitate the development of a rival company which could challenge what was a virtual monopoly in the limestone trade.

The road to Knowlbank Farm (Consall) in 1975. This embankment was originally raised to carry the North Stafford Railway of 1815. *Author*

The tunnel at Tunnel Farm (Wetley Rocks) in 1975, which perhaps would be best classified as an underbridge. It dates from 1815–16 and carried the turnpike road over the North Stafford Railway. *Author*

The gentlemen of the railway company remained undaunted, signed their agreement with the Marquis of Stafford and started to build the tramroad.[9] But there was another and more serious problem to be overcome. It appears that the partners never had sufficient funds to finance the railway scheme and with hopes of a link with the company's railway fading, new investors were hardly likely to take a risk. At this point fortune appeared to smile on the concern as an Act of Parliament was passed in 1817, by which Exchequer Bills could be issued to help with the construction of such works as railways. The Minutes of the Exchequer Loan Commissioners include:

> 24th July, 1817. Loan Application No. 84 from George Lambert Clifford: £8,000 to compleat [sic] the North Stafford Railway. Referred to the Committee.[10]

By this time, the tramroad had been built between Consall Forge and a point in the wood known as Cresswell's Piece (near Moorville Hall); which left a two mile stretch to be constructed to take the railway up to Weston Coyney. Little time seems to have been wasted in building this first section for the railway was completed to Lime Wharf Bank (on the modern A52) by September 1816. The mention of the railway and the lime wharf show that the line was operational by that date. The trustees were considering putting chains across the turnpike road at this point, so construction work must have been going on to the south of the road even if the traffic in lime was still limited.[11]

A week after receiving the application a loan of £8,000 was approved on the personal security of the partners and 'an Assignment of the property of the said Concern and all Profits and Advantages to be derived therefrom, [to] be taken as a Collateral Security'. The loan was for a period of three years and the partnership was listed as follows:

> Sir Thomas Hugh Clifford, Bart., of Tixall
> John Leigh of Consall Hall
> Walter Hill Coyney of Weston Coyney
> Walter Weston Coyney of Weston Coyney
> George Lambert Clifford of Foxearth House.[12]

The sum lent to the partnership seems to have been rather excessive if it was intended to use it to construct the remaining two miles of track over relatively easy ground. (An identical sum was sufficient to pay for the six mile stretch of the Hay Railway, between Hay and Eardisley.)[13] Possibly, the money was being used to pay existing debts; or was intended to finance the second phase of the North Stafford Railway scheme. This involved extending the railway from Consall Forge across the canalised section of the River Churnet and up through the Coombes Valley to Mixon Hay.[14] Exactly how much work was done on this side of the river remains uncertain, but the track is still traceable from Mosslee Mill to the Coombes Nature Reserve where stone blocks may still be seen. What does appear certain is that this section was never completed and therefore carried no traffic.[15]

The loan was due for repayment by 25th September, 1820, but in July the railway company made application for an extension. This was granted but

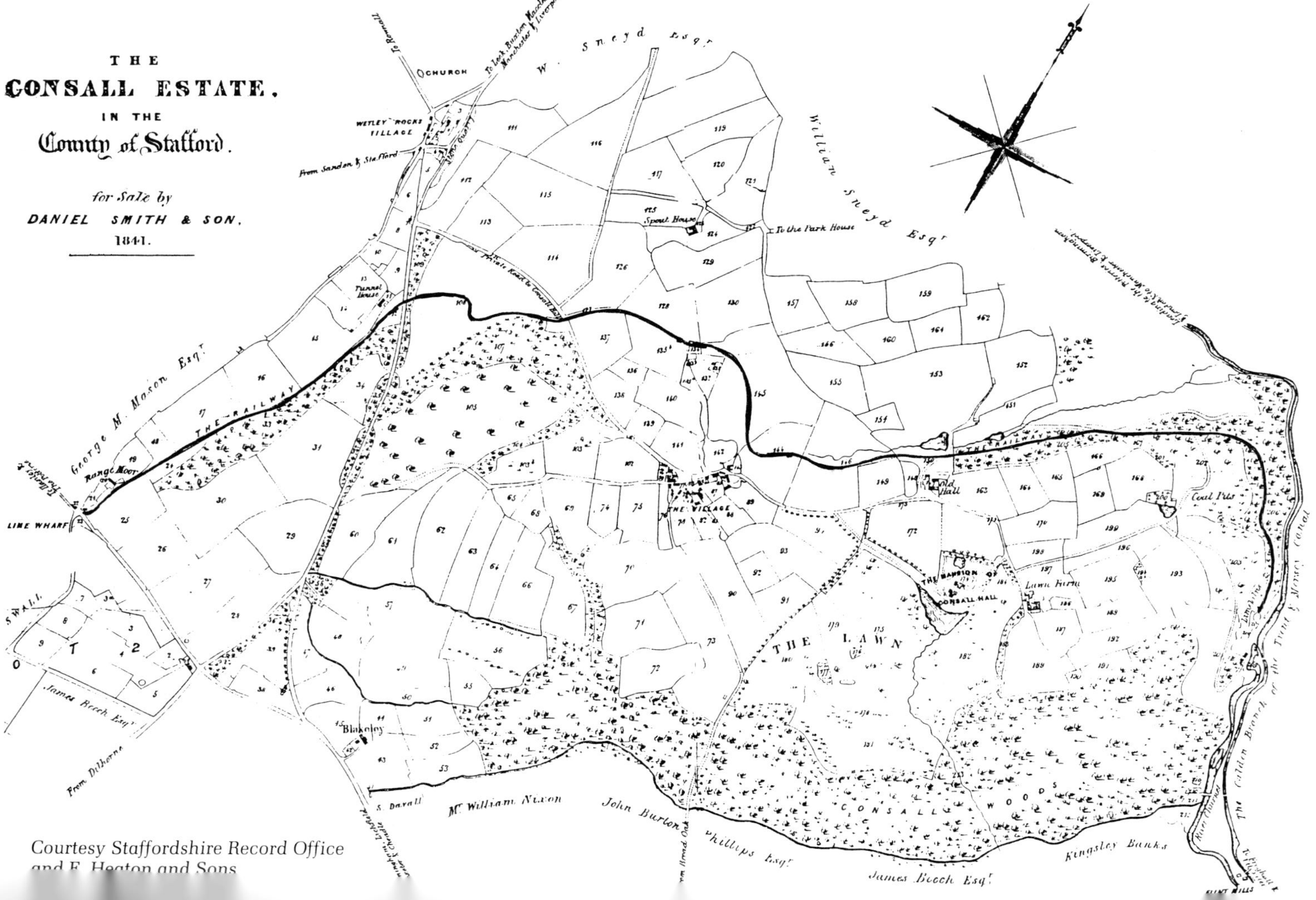

Courtesy Staffordshire Record Office and F. Heaton and Sons

the Exchequer Loan Commissioners considered:

> ... the Railway to have disappointed the expectations of the projectors, and not likely to prove beneficial, and they recommend the Board not to entertain any application for a further Loan should such be made.[16]

Despite this doleful assessment there seems to have been quite a lively trade in limestone along the recently completed tramroad and along both the Caldon and Uttoxeter Canals. In March 1819 the company were advertising 'lime of a very superior quality from Caldon Low Lime-stone ... delivered from covered boats, at any place along the line of the canals'. They gave their address as 'Lane End' (Longton), although this does not prove that they had any sort of office there.[17] Comparatively little is known of the company's activities between 1820 and 1830, but at best they were just keeping their heads above water. They did manage to attract one other investor into the partnership in the form of one Edward Hebdin, but he severed his connection in December 1820. The company also tried to open up a trade in stone gate posts from the quarries at Consall Forge, offering them for sale in July 1821 at the 'Cellar-Head and Weston Coyney' wharves.[18]

The company managed to repay its loan in October 1825[19], but the following extracts from a document of 1832 disclose the decline in the partnership:

> Whereas the said John Leigh and Walter Hill Coyney together with Sir Thomas Hugh Clifford and Walter Weston Coyney, George Lambert Clifford and Edward Hebdin Edquires did by certain articles of agreement dated 8th day of September become co-partners in the Business of Lime burning and in making and conducting a Railway from the Canal at Consall Wood to Lane End in the same county of Stafford and from Consall Wood aforesaid to Mixon Hay in the same county and for other purposes in the Articles mentioned for the terms of — years therein specified under the style of the North Stafford Railway Company. And whereas the said Sir Thomas Hugh Clifford and Edward Hebdin afterwards withdrew from the said Co-partnership and the Business was carried on by the other Co-partners under the same Firm. And whereas the said Co-partnership was dissolved some time ago or ceased to trade as a company when it was agreed that the said John Leigh should take to his own use all the Partnership stock, Book Debts and effects and pay and discharge these with or out of his own proper monies all Debts and demands of every description due and owing during the said Co-partnership.
> ... and he (John Leigh) was to receive the sum of £3,000 from the said Walter Hill Coyney to aid and assist him in paying such debts and demands and a further sum from the said G.L. Clifford which latter sum was duly paid him.
> ... Walter Weston Coyney now deceased, the late son of the said Walter Hill Coyney.
> ... Walter Hill Coyney being unable to raise and pay the said sum of £3,000 hath compounded with the said John Leigh and hath this day paid to him the sum of £1,500 — in full satisfaction and discharge of his debts in the North Stafford Railway Company.[20]

Shortly afterwards, William White records, Walter Hill Coyney leased out his home at Weston Coyney Hall and went to reside in France, where the cost of living was less.[21] A map published in 1832 shows that parts of the tramroad had already been abandoned and that Lime Wharf Bank (Cellarhead) was then the southern terminus. This explains a local tradition that the railway never extended beyond this point, although the advertisement of 1821 provides irrefutable evidence that the line was built as far as Weston Coyney. The testimony of the map is confirmed by a document of 1835 which describes the tramroad as 'communicating with the Turnpike Road leading to the Potteries'. It adds that this 'private Railway belonging to Mr Leigh' was used to carry lime, marl and other manures for 'the supply of a considerable district of the Country'.[22] So it is clear that nearly half of the tramroad was abandoned by 1832 and the other half taken over by John Leigh.

Leigh himself was declared bankrupt in 1840 and died in the following year. Many of his business interests were acquired by William Bowers of Cheadle, hence the erroneous local tradition that a 'Mr Lee and a Mr Bowers' built the tramroad.[23] A few years before Leigh's death: 'the Railway, Buildings, Waggons, 7 Lime Kilns at £250 per annum and 20 years purchase (in which the Stone Quarries are included)' were valued at £5,000. (This was actually a reduced valuation.) There is no evidence to suggest that the tramroad was used after 1840, although evidence collected by Johnstone indicated that it closed between 1846 and 1850. It was certainly derelict by 1856 when it is referred to in a lease as 'the way from the old limekilns up past Consall Hall, to Consall village'.[24]

During his fieldwork excursions Johnstone discovered a number of cast-iron plate rails. Other examples of such rails have survived and they have proved to be identical to the rails used on the Caldon Low (1804) and the Woodhead (1809) tramroads. Indeed the present author took a rail from the Woodhead line in 1976 and matched it to stone blocks still *in situ* near Lime Wharf Bank, Cellarhead. All the rails are of a pattern produced by the Butterley Iron Company, although Philip Riden who has made a study of the company, was unable to trace any record of a relevant transaction. Identical examples may be seen at the Cheddleton Flint Mill Museum and these bear interesting casting marks. As John Leigh once operated the Cheddleton Mills it is likely that he had the rails brought here, perhaps from an abandoned section of the North Stafford Railway. It now seems likely that all these rails were 'pirate rails', manufactured to the Butterley pattern by some local ironworks. An unusual feature of the track of both the North Stafford Railway and the Woodhead tramroad is that some of the stone blocks were plugged with lead, rather than the more customary wooden pegs. According to the late Bertram Baxter, the only other tramroad to use this type of plug was that built by the Sirhowy Company who obtained their rails from the Butterley Company.[25] Another interesting aspect of the wayleave agreement is that provision was made for waggons 'to be moved by any Invention or Device'. Perhaps if the company had been allowed to realise its greater plan, then this might have been the first line in North Staffordshire to employ stationary or even locomotive steam engines.[26]

References

1. J.D. Johnstone, *Werrington: Some Notes on its History*, (1946), pp. 35–41. An edited version was reprinted as 'The Consall Plateway', in *The Railway Magazine*, January/February 1949, pp. 14–16.
2. SRO: D593/T/7/1.
3. SRO: D593/K/1/5/4 (7th March, 1815).
4. J.R. Wordie, op. cit., p. 62.
5. SRO: D593/K/1/5/4.
6. SRO: D239/M/1023 (2nd March, 1832).
7. SRO: D593/K/1/5/4 (27th May, 1815).
8. Information from Mr H.L. Podmore.
9. SRO: D593/K/1/5/4 (5th June, 1815).
10. PRO: PWLB 2/1. (Information provided by Grahame Boyes.)
11. *Staffordshire Advertiser*, 14th September, 1816.
12. PRO: PWLB 2/1 (31st July, 1817).
13. Information from Gordon Rattenbury.
14. SRO: D234/M/1023.
15. *Leek Post and Times*, 11th January, 1978.
16. PRO: PWLB 2/3 (27th July, 7th September and 19th October, 1820).
17. *Staffordshire Advertiser*, 20th March, 1819.
18. Ibid., 9th December, 1820 and 14th July, 1821.
19. PRO: PWLB 2/5 (6th October, 1825).
20. SRO: D239/M/1023.
21. William White, op. cit., p. 731.
22. J. Phillips and W.F. Hutchings, *A Map of the County of Stafford*, (1832) (The survey was made in 1831–1832); and SRO: D593/V/5/49.
23. J.D. Johnstone, 'Consall Plateway', loc. cit., p. 16.
24. SRO: D1176/B/3/11 and SRO: D239/M/1065.
25. Bertram Baxter, *Stone Blocks and Iron Rails (Tramroads)*, (1966), p. 51.
26. SRO: D593/T/7/1.

A close-up of the rail placed on the blocks at Rangemoor in 1975. Note the distinctive 'toe' adjacent to the flange. *Author*

Bibliography

Books and Directories

John Aikin, *A Description of the Country from Thirty to Forty Miles Round Manchester* (London, 1795)
Bertram Baxter, *Stone Blocks and Iron Rails* (Newton Abbot, 1966)
Anne Bayliss, *The Life and Works of James Trubshaw* (Stockport, 1978)
Harold Bode, *The Leek Canal and Rudyard Reservoir* (Leek, 1984)
William Chapman, *Observations on the various systems of Canal Navigation* (London, 1797)
Herbert A. Chester, *The Iron Valley* (Cheadle, 1979)
Herbert A. Chester, *Cheadle: Coal Town* (Cheadle, 1981)
Rex Christiansen and R.W. Miller, *The North Staffordshire Railway* (Newton Abbot, 1971)
Robert Copeland, *A short history of pottery raw materials and the Cheddleton Flint Mill* (Cheddleton, 1972)
John Farey, *Agriculture and Minerals of Derbyshire* (London, 1817)
Katherine Eufemia Farrer, *Correspondence of Josiah Wedgwood* (1906)
Charles Hadfield, *Canals of the West Midlands* (Newton Abbot, 1969)
Charles Hadfield, *British Canals* (Newton Abbot, 1984)
Leslie James, *A Chronology of the Construction of Britain's Railways, 1778–1855* (London, 1983)
Alan Jeffery, *The Caldon Canal* (Leek, 1971)
J.D. Johnstone, *Werrington: Some Notes on its History* (Cheadle, 1946)
Joseph Kennedy (Ed.), *Biddulph: A Local History* (Keele, 1980)
Robert Keys, *The Churnet Valley Railway*, (Hartington, 1974)
Peter Lead, *The Trent and Mersey Canal*, (Ashbourne, 1980)
M.J.T. Lewis, *Early Wooden Railways* (London, 1970)
Roy Lewis, *Directories of Cheadle* (Stafford, 1971)
Jean Lindsay, *The Trent and Mersey Canal* (Newton Abbot, 1979)
Robert Milner (Ed.), *Cheddleton: A village history* (Cheddleton, 1983)
John Morton, *Thomas Bolton and Sons Limited* (Ashbourne, 1983)
W. Parson and T. Bradshaw, *Staffordshire: General and Commercial Directory* (1818)
Joseph Priestley, *Navigable Rivers, Canals and Railways* (London, 1831)
Francis Redfern, *History of Uttoxeter* (Hanley, 1886)
Philip Riden, *The Butterley Company, 1790–1830* (Wingerworth, 1973)
Henry de Salis, *Bradshaw's Canals and Navigable Rivers* (London, 1904)
Simeon Shaw, *History of the Staffordshire Potteries* (Hanley, 1829)
Samuel Smiles, *Lives of the Engineers*, Vol. 1 (London, 1862)
Robert Speake (Ed.), *The Old Road to Endon* (Keele, 1974)
John Thomas, *The Rise of the Staffordshire Potteries* (Bath, 1971)
W.G. Torrance, *Following Francis Redfern* (Uttoxeter, 1974)
John Ward, *History of the Borough of Stoke-upon-Trent* (London, 1843)
William White, *Directory of Staffordshire* (1834)
J. Ross Wordie, *Estate Management in Eighteenth-Century England* (London 1982)

Articles

S.H. Beaver, 'The Potteries: A Study in the Evolution of a Cultural Landscape', *Trans. Inst. British Geographers*, No. 34 (1964).

W.H. Chaloner, 'James Brindley and his remuneration as a Canal Engineer', *Trans. of the Lancashire and Cheshire Antiquarian Society*, Vols 75 and 76 (1965–66).

A.E. and E.M. Dodd, 'The Froghall–Uttoxeter Canal', *North Staffordshire Journal of Field Studies*, Vol. 3 (1963).

J.R. Hollick, 'The Caldon Low Tramways', *Railway Magazine*, June 1937.

J.D. Johnstone, 'The Consall Plateway', *Railway Magazine*, January/February 1949.

Peter Lead and John Robey, 'Steam Power in North Staffordshire, 1750–1850', *JSIAS*, No. 9 (1980).

Peter Lead and Hugh Torrens, 'Richard Trevithick, The Heath Family and the North Staffordshire Connection', *Jn. Trevithick Society*, No. 10 (1983).

Hugh Torrens, 'The Somersetshire Coal Canal Caisson Lock', *Bristol Industrial Archaeological Society Journal*, (1975).

In 1976, Colin and Pat Walker attempted to re-introduce the old trade in coal. They are seen here making deliveries at Denford. *Author*

Index

Alton 60–1, 66
Ashbourne Canal (Proposed) 58, 60, 63
Bagnall Reservoir 21, 34
Banks, Sir Joseph 7
Beatrice 40, 42
Beaver, S.H. 30
Bill, Charles 60
Bill, Robert 13
Bill, William 17, 19, 22
Billings, John 75, 80
Birches Head 11
Birdswood 46–7
Boatyards 27, 63
Bobs 80–1
Bolton, Thomas & Sons 37–40, 42–3
Bowers, William 36, 65, 92
Bridgewater, Duke of 7, 28, 57
Brindley, James 7, 46, 50
Brunner-Mond 36–7, 40
Caisson lock (proposed) 30
Caldon Canal Society 41–6
Caldon Lime Company 25
Caldon Low Railways 34, 67–84
Caldon Low Quarries 7, 13, 33–4, 63, 76, 78–9, 80–3
Cast-iron aqueduct 65
Cellarhead Wharf 84, 89, 91–2
Cheadle Brass Company 60, 63
Cheddleton 26, 34
Cheddleton Flint Mills 12, 20, 28, 34, 92
Cheddleton Lime Company 19, 25
Cheddleton Paper Mills 24, 30, 37
Cherryeye Bridge 35
Clifford, George Lambert 85–9
Cockshead Colliery 25, 27–8, 52
Coleman, J.H. 37
Commercial Canal Scheme 51, 57–8
Consall Estate 90
Consall Forge 19, 29, 85
Consall Mills 19, 25, 28, 34
Coombes Valley 37, 38, 89
Copestake, Henry 13, 72
Coyney, Walter Hill 89, 91
Coyney, Walter Weston 89, 91
Crumpwood Weir 56, 65
Denford 33
Donnington Wood Canal 10, 69
Dukart, Davis 10
Eagle Pottery 11, 30, 37
Endon Tip 16, 18, 37
Engine Lock 27–8, 52
Etruria 5
Etruria Vale Mill 8, 37
Farey, John 17, 53, 69, 72–6
Farmer's Friend 32, 36
Foxley Branch Canal 37
Frog 80
Froghall Tunnel 45–6
Froghall Wharf 23, 40, 48–9, 67, 74
Froghall Wharf Passenger Service 46

Gilbert, John (Senior) 3, 7, 10, 22, 25, 27, 50, 67–9
Gilbert, John (Junior) 25, 27, 50, 57
Gilbert, Thomas 3, 7, 17, 19, 21, 22, 30–1, 57, 67, 72
Gresley, Sir Nigel Bowyer 57
Hadfield, Charles 17–9, 54
Haematite 33–6
Havelock 16, 40
Hazelhurst 33, 53, 56
Henshall, Hugh 10, 12, 46, 51, 69
Hollick, Dr J.R. 67
Iron boats 27
Johnson Brothers 8–9, 44
Knypersley Reservoir 21, 23, 25, 34
Leek Canal 51–5, 64
Leek Tunnel 54–5
Leek Wharf 54–5
Leigh, John 28–30, 63–5, 87–92
Lily of the Lake 40
Limekilns 23, 26–7, 63, 87
Loch, James 85–7
Meakin, J. & G. 2, 37
Milton Maid 9, 44–6
Milton Princess 46
Milton Queen 8, 9, 44
Nora 40
North Stafford Railway Company (1815–32) 54, 84–93
North Staffordshire Railway and Canal Company 33, 37, 65, 78, 80
Norton Branch Canal 19, 34, 52
Norton Ironworks 37
Oakamoor 61
Perpetual 24, 36–7
Podmore, William and Sons 37
Potter, James 25, 53
Rennie, John 23, 28, 30, 51, 58, 70, 72–6
Robinson, William 21, 57, 76, 87
Rudyard Reservoir 23, 51–3
Sneyd, Edward 17–9
Sneyd, John 7
Sparrow, John 19, 22, 25, 27
Sparrow, Thomas 23
Stafford, Marquis of 85–9
Stanley Pool 21, 34
Stoke Boat Club 41
Telford, Thomas 25
Toad 80–1, 83
Tolls 17–8, 23, 25, 64
Trubshaw, James 25, 78
Uttoxeter Canal 53, 56–66
Uttoxeter Wharf 61–5
Water Supply – problems 21
Wedgwood, Josiah I 7, 12, 21, 28, 46
Wedgwood, Josiah II 27, 57–8
Weldon, Robert 30–1
Weston Coyney Wharf 84–9
Woodhead Colliery Company 36, 53
Woodhead Tramroad 59, 62–5, 92